DETOURS &
DESTINATIONS

DETOURS &
DESTINATIONS

Vicki Borders

XULON PRESS

Xulon Press
2301 Lucien Way #415
Maitland, FL 32751
407.339.4217
www.xulonpress.com

Unless otherwise indicated, Scripture quotations taken from the Holy Bible, New International Version (NIV). Copyright © 1973, 1978, 1984, 2011 by Biblica, Inc.™. Used by permission. All rights reserved.

Scripture quotations taken from the King James Version (KJV)–*public domain.*

Printed in the United States of America.

ISBN-13: 978-1-6305-0944-6

Unless otherwise indicated, Scripture verses are taken from the Holy Bible, New International Version.

Table of Contents

Dedication

This book is dedicated to the One who knew me even before I was knit together in my mother's womb. Thank you, Lord. In my meager human efforts, you are so worthy of anything I try to write, about how truly great You are. This book is also dedicated to my husband and my family, who I cherish beyond words. Without you, I would have no story. Thank you for the love and support you surround me with on this journey called life.

Introduction

There's an old Nancy Sinatra song from the 1970s that says "We got married in a fever, hotter than a pepper sprout. We've been talking' bout Jackson, ever since the fire went out."

In 1972, at the ripe old age of nineteen, I married Mr. Linsey Borders in a fever as hot as a jalapeño. We didn't go to Jackson, but we had a hot destination. It was Honolulu Hawaii, where we began a life of moving! In forty-seven years of marriage, we packed up and moved nineteen times. We lived in twelve different cities/towns in six different states. We owned eleven homes, not to mention the rentals. We never became especially well-traveled, but we did become masters at packing boxes and loading U-Haul trucks. We learned right from the start, that life IS a journey!

We were not following the Lord Jesus Christ from the very beginning, but He was watching and guiding us. In His sovereignty, He knew that we needed to get used to a lifestyle that would never allow any moss to grow under our feet. If we all could truly comprehend the fact that we are merely sojourners, just passing through until we make the "ultimate" journey, we could spare ourselves so much stress, anxiety and heartache.

We could trust more, love more and forgive more, grasping the abundant life that Jesus intended for us to live. We could have more joy. "I have come that they may have life, and have it to the full," Jesus said in John 10:10.

"Follow Me," He says. I am here to tell you that Jesus IS worth following. He is a gracious, loving leader. In John 14:6, He said "I am the way and the truth and the life. No one comes to the Father, except through Me."

How I wish I would have chosen to follow Him sooner. He spoke to me many times in earlier years. I made some crazy turns and detours, but He was faithful, never allowing me to get so far off course that I could not find my way. You do realize, don't you, that you can never get so lost that you cannot find your way to Him? He'll always be waiting for you, just as He was for me, with arms open wide, saying "Come to Me, child. I will never leave you or forsake you." He is my "GPS." That is, my Great Personal Savior. It's been a wild trip and it's not over yet!

Chapter One

I was born and raised in a little town just outside of Kent, Ohio, home of Kent State University, and I am an ORIGINAL. Not a copy, not a "wannabe," but an original product of the "love generation." That is, hippies, bell bottoms, flower power, peace signs, protestors and coffee houses. Back then, Kent State was as much a part of the hippie cult as UC Berkeley was, out in California. Me? I was really quite a part of it all. I don't know where I really stood on any of the issues of the day. Frankly, I think I wanted to make more of a fashion statement, with my long hair, beads and peace signs. I was a rebel without a cause.

There was a group back then that did have a great cause. They were called the "Jesus Freaks." They went around telling people about the Lord, because they had figured out that you really could have peace and love, but the source of that peace and love came from knowing Jesus Christ in a personal way. I didn't know Jesus then. I wish I would have, though, and I wonder how He would have used me, had I truly been His child.

Those were the "good old days"! I thought I had my life planned out. Those plans included me attending Kent State to major in art. Just before I graduated from high school, however, four students lost their lives in a confrontation with the National Guard on that campus, during a Vietnam War protest rally. How sad to look back and realize that this was, perhaps, the very first nationally publicized school shooting. We never dreamed that we'd go on to live in a world where tragedies like this would become horribly common place. This was not common place then though, and my mother said "over her dead body" would I attend Kent State. My mother and I weren't close, but I could not fight her on this decision. I had no money. If I would have been a straight A student, perhaps I could have followed my real dream of becoming a veterinarian, but I was just an average student.

I'd already lost my father. He was killed in a car accident on his way home from work one morning, when I was only thirteen. In my young mind, I felt that it had been my fault. I usually walked to school, but on the morning of the accident it was very cold outside, and I'd been sick. I was waiting for him to return home from work so he could take me to school. I thought that maybe he could have been rushing home because of me. Perhaps, I thought, if that hadn't been the case, he might have passed by the scene of the accident a few seconds later and the calamity could have been avoided. I hardly knew my father. He worked nights and slept days, so I only saw him on the weekends, plus one week each summer when we took a family vacation. Even though we weren't close, he treated my mother kindly and modeled to me how a man should treat his wife. When he died, I lost that example at such a crucial age. I never recovered from the void his death created, until I met the Lord Jesus Christ, many years later.

You may be fatherless too, whether from death, divorce or estrangement, and I'll bet you know exactly what I'm talking about. Do you ever feel a twinge of sadness when you see someone with a warm, loving relationship with their father? That's how I felt. The Lord began to heal that pain when I discovered some of His words on this subject. Jeremiah 49:11 says

"Leave your orphans; I will protect their lives. Your widows too can trust in Me." In Psalm 10:14b He said "You are the helper of the fatherless." I didn't know it then, but one day I would have a warm, loving relationship with the Father of ALL fathers.

My mother was a no-nonsense, work-oriented soul, and I was a "free spirit," so we didn't see eye-to-eye on anything. I know she loved me, but I never heard the words or received much affection of any kind. She went to work full time after dad died, and as long as I did my chores to her exact specifications, we got along well enough. I couldn't wait to leave home. She took the agony of her loss out on me. On one occasion, I had neglected to clean the bathroom just right, and she began to beat me. I was strong enough to hold her wrists to protect myself. She was in such a rage that she made a telephone call, in my presence, to a local children's home. From her end of the conversation, it was clear that she was trying to arrange for them to come and pick me up. I began to scream and sob and beg her to end the call, promising to try harder to accomplish all that she expected of me. It wasn't until years later that I realized she had been speaking to a "dial tone," intent on punishing me. She succeeded. It was the cruelest thing she ever did, and I remained deeply wounded for many years.

Chapter Two

With my hopes of attending Kent State University dashed, I had no idea what to do. The Lord knew I needed some education and He knew I needed a job. A close friend of mine decided to attend an airline school in Hartford, Connecticut, and my mother miraculously agreed to allow me to go with her. It was a detour from my original plans, but I was so ready to go anywhere. The goal of the school was to train students to find employment with the airlines as ticket agents, reservationists and travel agents. Just before graduation, however, the first national airline strike made the news. No airlines were hiring and our hopes were not going to materialize. Several government agencies came to our school to do some recruiting, among them the FBI and the CIA. Our government was looking for women willing to move to our nation's capitol. This looked to be a very exciting career and a new beginning for me, so I signed up. Can you imagine giving a Top Secret security clearance to a "flower child"? No wonder this country was such a mess! It took three months to get my security clearance, and then off I went to Washington, D.C. to work for the Central Intelligence Agency.

Washington was a fast-paced place to live, with so much nightlife, so many parties and so much to do. Soon I was right in the middle of it all, drunk on my independence. The Bible

4

says in Hebrews 11:25 that there's pleasure in sin for a short time, and that's true. Eventually though, the thrill wore off. I was ready for a change and an escape from my lifestyle. Amidst work, and all the socializing, deep inside I was a very lonely soul. I felt unloved, even though I could be the life of the party. No one was trying to point me to Jesus. If they were, I was not interested. God, in all His goodness and mercy, saw my longing. He had a very special appointment planned for me. He was about to show me His plans for a brand new destination.

In March of 1972, three of my girlfriends from Ohio came to visit. My two roommates and I were so excited to show them all the national monuments and, of course, the great night spots that we all frequented. There was one place in particular that we loved, called "The Bayou." They always had a live band and they had a large dance floor. The six of us arrived early and found a table. Right after the band started, Mr. Linsey Borders came over and asked me to dance. Linsey had just left the U.S. Naval Academy in Annapolis, Maryland, and was temporarily stationed in Washington, awaiting further Naval orders. After a couple of dances, he seated himself with all of us and we talked the entire evening. He insisted that he be our tour guide for the weekend. He was a little wild and crazy, but there was enough of Jesus shining through him that I knew there was something different about this guy, and I was interested.

We'd only been dating for three months when he received his Naval orders to Pearl Harbor, Hawaii. It was either get married, or never see each other again. We decided to take the chance. He left for Hawaii, and I resigned my job and quickly moved back to Ohio, where I planned a small, very speedy wedding for September 23, 1972, which was exactly six months to the day after we met.

Our wedding was nice, but very simple. I wanted so much to play my guitar and sing a song that I'd written for my husband-to-be, but I allowed my mother to talk me out of it. I had arranged for a folk duo, friends from Washington, to sing, but during the week of our wedding, Congress called an emergency session and one of the girls was required to work. So, other than the "Wedding March," we had no music at all. This is the song that I wrote to my wonderful husband:

THURSDAYS

by Vicki Borders
1972

Today the world's so busy, every day goes by so fast, that before we finish Monday, another week has passed
And me, I'm always busy too, but on one day I slow down, and the world, it just can't rush me, on that day I call my own.

I was born on Thursday night, in a cold and gray December
But that's not why it's Thursday, I always will remember
It all began that Thursday night, the night you took a chance and walked up to me shyly and asked me for a dance.

As we danced you smiled at me, I couldn't help but smile too. The music must have read my mind as it drew me near to you. I'll never know what told me so but before the dance was through,
I had the strangest feeling, I'd fall in love with you.

Thursdays came and Thursdays went, still we shared our smiles,
picnicking upon a hill, or driving miles and miles
We shared our secrets, hopes and dreams, we even shared our
tears, and though the days weren't many, to us they seemed
like years

And it was on a Thursday night, beneath the sky so blue, you
asked if I would be your wife and share my life with you

I'll always be your listening ear and I'll warm you when
you're cold
Together we will walk life's roads, and together we'll grow old
On trust and understanding, we'll place our highest worth and
the love we share between us will circle round the earth.

I thank the Lord for Mondays, Tuesdays, Wednesdays too...but
I love the Lord for Thursdays, cause on Thursday,
He brought you

Linsey loved that song. Music or no music, we were officially
Mr. and Mrs. Linsey Borders.

Chapter Three

We spent the next three years honeymooning in beautiful Hawaii. We thoroughly enjoyed the island life. We basked in the sun, swam and snorkeled at the beautiful beaches, learned to eat with chop sticks and love the local food and entertainment. Surprisingly, just as I arrived on Oahu, there was an opening at the CIA office there. Linsey was still on leave, and one afternoon we'd been to the beach. When we arrived back at our apartment, there was a business card slipped under our front door, asking me to meet a gentleman at the top of the Ilikai Hotel, in Waikiki, for an interview. The funny thing is, Linsey had only found that apartment days before our wedding and, as far as we knew, no one knew the address. Hmmm. I was hired, so I was able to continue my work for our government.

We lived four different places in Honolulu. Our favorite was a beautiful condo on the side of "Punchbowl," a mountain which is really a crater, covered with lush green vegetation, homes and condos. We could sit on our lanai and watch the beautiful sunsets and see the ocean from afar. What a life! We were not permitted to own pets there, however, and being the animal lover that I was, I wanted a puppy so badly. Eventually, we moved from this picturesque setting to a very basic duplex on a busy street with no view. It was, however, equipped with a back yard for our "new baby."

He was an Old English Sheepdog puppy named Sherlock. He was a large, frolicking, shaggy, gray and white, exuberant, life-loving fur ball. He was totally worth the move and he became such a part of our lives from the very beginning. He loved the beach as much as we did and he could body surf! We both had grown up attending church, but that had not yet become a desire of ours. One Easter Sunday, we thought it might be nice to go to a sunrise service overlooking Hanauma Bay. Hanauma Bay is a gorgeous sea life preserve, known for its beauty and amazing snorkeling opportunities. We stood overlooking the ocean and watched the sun come up. The pastor was telling us about Jesus, and how He died for us, and that He rose again and that we could begin a personal relationship with Him. He said we could have our sins forgiven and know that we have eternal life. He invited whoever would, to step forward and make a commitment and pray with him. At the church I attended during my childhood, I did not remember ever hearing that I could really "know" Christ. This man made Jesus sound like a real person who was totally approachable, someone who I'd completely missed out on getting to know. I felt so emotional about this and about the possibility that per-haps God really loved me. I felt moved to step forward and make that commitment, but I was embarrassed, so I stood my ground, refusing the Lord. A seed was planted in my heart that day though. I did not forget what I had heard.

Chapter Four

A fter nearly three years in Hawaii, Linsey left the Navy and we moved back to Ohio, where it was Linsey who attended Kent State University. I found what I thought was a good job as a legal secretary, near the university. What I didn't learn until after I was hired, was that this law firm, comprised of four attorneys, went through secretaries like piranhas in a feeding frenzy! I had been the tenth secretary hired in less than a year. It was not uncommon to be sworn at, demeaned in the presence of clients, and have files literally thrown at me. What completely baffled me was the dogged determination of my co-worker to endure their treatment. She'd been with them for several years. She was a younger, single gal whose self-control and maturity greatly surpassed her age.

She had recently become engaged. She was planning a big, beautiful wedding and she often shared with me how her plans were coming together. She was filled with love for her fiancé. She was bubbling with joy and expectation for the life she would soon be sharing with her new husband. I knew she was a believer in Jesus Christ because she occasionally talked about her faith. One day after the attorneys had reached new heights in their rudeness and crudeness, even she was thoroughly exasperated. She began to rant, and expressed to me that she would give up everything, including her upcoming marriage, if the

Lord Jesus Christ would return. She was deadly serious and I was dumbfounded that anyone would want to forego life and love for Jesus. That was total CRAZY talk, as far as I was concerned.

It was only a few months later that we both reached our saturation point with this job. Since she was our office manager and authorized to do so, she wrote us each our final paycheck and we left those men a "Dear John" letter, slid the office keys under door, went to lunch and never came back. We couldn't get out of there fast enough, but not before God had a chance to water the seeds that He had planted in my heart through the pastor in Hawaii, about the merits of the love of Christ and the dedication He receives from those who diligently follow Him.

We were soon able to buy our first home. It was a small, two acre farm. I'd never felt more at peace. Being a country girl was my destiny. I could have stayed there forever. It became the place where I would be able to own my first horse. In addition to dogs, I had loved horses since I was a two year old and was placed upon the back of one of my grandfather's huge work horses. As a toddler, I was known to break tiny model horses by sitting on them, pretending to ride. As I grew a little older, I could be seen running around our backyard, prancing and whinnying, "holding my reins," pretending to be both horse and rider, as I galloped to imaginary destinations. Our neighbors must have shook their heads and whispered to each other about that poor afflicted child.

You can't imagine how excited I was to be able to sign up for riding lessons at a stable near the university and really learn to ride correctly. I became more smitten than ever with horses and the dream of owning my own. I was working full-time and we were meeting all of our obligations. Could we afford a horse? I'd waited my whole life. Through a friend of a friend, we found out about one that was for sale at a price we could afford. This horse was hand-picked by God. His name was Captain Fox and he was a thirteen year old Morgan gelding. Captain was fearless, completely kind, and beautiful. He loved to gallop as much as I did, with the wind blowing through his mane, and his hooves pounding the earth. We had so many adventures together and never could I have owned a more perfect "first horse."

Upon graduation from college, Linsey's new job presented us with another new destination, South Bend, Indiana. He had earned his Bachelor of Arts degree. I had earned my PHT, "Pushing Hubby Through". I felt both excited and conflicted. I loved our farm and all of our college friends, and I knew that this move would bring about many changes. I continued to feel this yearning in my soul. One afternoon shortly before we left, I walked out to the back of our pasture and sat by myself on a tree stump. I talked out loud to the Lord, something I had never done before. I asked Him if He would go with us to Indiana and be with us there. I sensed His presence. I still remembered what the pastor in Hawaii said, and I wondered if it was really possible to truly know Jesus.

It could have been the yearning. It could have been the reality that we were about to uproot ourselves again and a big "unknown" was looming out there. Whatever it was, my feelings spilled out onto paper. A new song was born, a needed balm for my soul.

BEFORE I'M THROUGH

By Vicki Borders

Sometimes I wish I could be satisfied
With all the things I have and with everything I've tried
But I've got to keep on moving, Lord, got to trust and follow You
Chasing every dream and every scheme cause
There's so much to do before I'm through

Life is so short and there's so little time
When you're young and you're strong and your spirit can fly
I've never lived life just halfway you know,
It's all the way whether smiles or tears
Just got to take some time and ease my mind
And figure out, where am I going from here?

Part of me wants to be a country girl,
Riding horses all day long
And I'd like to spend a while making people smile
Maybe traveling and singing my songs
And I'd like to settle down with the man I love
And have a baby, maybe two
Maybe with the good Lord willing, I can do it all
Before I'm through, before I'm through

Someday when I'm old, may I still give God praise
For each mercy encountered throughout all my days
For each precious dream that came to be
And for those left unfulfilled
Knowing He knew what was best for me
Safe within His loving will, to see and do before I'm through.

Chapter Five

S oon we packed up our things and all of our animals and arrived in South Bend. Linsey and I had now been married almost seven years, and we were very happy. We found an apartment for a short while, but eventually found a beautiful seven acre farm to rent. We really liked that farm and wanted to buy it, but the owners had no plans of selling, so we moved once more. Interestingly enough, a year or so later, we learned that the house burned to the ground from possible faulty wiring. God had protected us!

We bought our second home, in a subdivision, right down the street from Notre Dame University, where I worked part time in the Psychology Department. We could hear the marching band's fight song (Go Irish) from our house during the football games. We boarded Captain at a riding stable so close that I could ride my bicycle to get there. We made lots of new friends and Linsey really liked his job. I was still aware of this empty place in my heart, though, that even Linsey and the animals hadn't been able to fill. Maybe that's what I was feeling on that afternoon before our move, when, in the back of our pasture, I asked the Lord if He would go with us to Indiana. I didn't understand that there really is an empty place in every heart that can only be filled by the Lord Jesus Christ.

I began to look back over my life and I could see all the near misses I'd had with tragedy and serious trouble, like I'd seen many of my friends encounter. I knew it could have easily been me. I believed that it had to have been God who had seen me through. I knew He existed. I had an excellent "head knowledge" of Him. I'd never cracked open a Bible and I rarely prayed, but I wanted to thank Him for all those times He watched over me and helped me to find such a loving husband and a happy life. The Bible says "Seek and you will find, knock and the door will be opened to you," in Luke 11:9. "You will seek Me and find Me when you seek Me with all your heart," it says in Jeremiah 29:13.

I convinced Linsey that we needed to start going to church. He wasn't excited about the idea at first, but he finally agreed. We visited all kinds of churches. The Lord soon honored my seeking, searching heart and He led us to a church where the Pastor there came out to our home one evening and opened up the Bible and showed me right from God's word that I could have my past totally forgiven, I could start all over again with a clean slate, and I could have eternal life. I had to believe, and say a prayer, and mean it with all of my heart. "For God so loved the world that He gave His one and only Son, that whoever believes in Him may have eternal life," it says in John 3:16. Romans 10:13 says "Everyone who calls on the name of the Lord will be saved." It was because of the indescribable love of Jesus that I was made spiritually alive by His sacrifice on the cross. He died for me, slaying the sin in my life, giving me a vision of heaven and filling me with a peace that passed all understanding. I was so ready to get to know this Jesus. There was no turning back. I called upon the Lord and I was radically saved! This is the first song I wrote after the best decision I ever made.

I CHOOSE YOU, LORD

by Vicki Borders

I choose you, Lord to be my God and king
Friend and helper, Master of everything
From the shadow of Your wings to Your mighty hand I'll cling
I choose You, Lord, I choose You.

I choose you, Lord please guide me as I grow
Teach me forgiveness toward both friend and foe
By my example may all around me know
That I choose You Lord, I choose You

You called out to me when I was lost
And so far from Your will
When You gave Your life
My name was on Your mind
My sweetest song could not express the gratitude I feel
Nor could anything I say or do repay this debt I owe to You

I choose you, Lord, the life, the truth, the way
Make me a seeker of lost sheep gone astray
Give me the courage to always boldly say
Why I choose You, Lord, I choose You
I choose You, Lord, I choose You.

Chapter Six

L ife was so exciting as a new Christian. My heart began to change immediately. 2 Corinthians 5:17 says "Therefore, if anyone is in Christ, he is a new creation. The old has gone, the new has come."

I was surprised to find that I was still searching. This time, though, I was searching for different things. I began to pray and read my Bible. It didn't always make sense, but I was learning that God had specific plans for my life. I came across a verse that said "But seek first His kingdom and His righteousness and all these things will be given to you as well," Matthew 6:33. I wanted everything I did to be in line with what God's plans were for my life. I knew I had taken too many detours in my past and had found myself so lost and confused. I now wanted God to direct my every step. "If the Lord delights in a man's way, He makes his steps firm," it says in Psalm 37:23. I had a list of "things" that I would love to have given to me, as that verse mentioned. Those things were maybe selfish things, or silly things, but they were very important things to me, that the Lord was totally aware of. As time began to pass and I began to grow as a Christian and learn to obey God more and more, God began to reward my obedience and go down my "list" and check those things off, one by one.

The number one item on my list then was my desire to become a mother. We had been married eight years. I had surrounded myself with my animal family from very early in our marriage. Animals love you unconditionally. Animals are not judgmental of your appearance or your status in life; they never want to leave you and they fill you with laughter and joy, daily, in the most amazing ways. My experiences in the realm of human family did not conjure up those same warm and fuzzy feelings. Linsey came from a large, loving family, however. I loved them all and I always enjoyed their get-togethers, and I knew that Linsey had a definite desire to have children.

As I grew in my relationship with the Lord, I began learning and seeing that, just like the relationship I had with my animals, God also loved me unconditionally. He too, was not judgmental of my appearance or of my status in life. He also promised never to leave me or forsake me and if I would allow it, He, too, would fill me with awe and joy daily in the most amazing ways. It was time for me to place my full trust in the Creator and not His creation. Maybe, just maybe, I thought, if we could have children and model our family according to God's blueprint, it could be a very happy and fulfilling experience. How thankful I was that we had not desired to start our family before we both came to know and love Jesus.

Chapter Seven

What a day it was when I learned I was pregnant. I was strong and healthy and had read that there was no reason not to continue to do the activities my body was used to doing, so I did not quit riding my horse. I didn't take a spill or overly exert myself, but my first pregnancy ended in a miscarriage. I do not know if riding really had anything to do with it, but I was shattered. How could God allow me to lose this baby when we'd been married so long and I finally had the desire to be a mom? This was my first real test from the Lord. James 1:2-4 says "Consider it pure joy, my brothers, whenever you face trials of many kinds, because you know that the testing of your faith develops perseverance. Perseverance must finish its work so that you may be mature and complete, not lacking anything." He never promised us that being a Christian was going to be a bowl full of cherries. I told Him I would follow Him, and that I believed His word and trusted Him to lead me. Would I still trust Him with hardship and loss?

He also allows these trials and tribulations into our lives so that we may comfort others when they go through them. For the first time in my new Christian life, I was approached by women in our church who had also lost babies. I didn't even know them. This was overwhelming to me, because they were reaching out, and sharing God's love with me. 2 Corinthians

1:3-4 says " Praise be to the God and Father of the Lord Jesus Christ, the Father of compassion and the God of all comfort, who comforts us in all our troubles, so that we can comfort those in any trouble with any comfort we ourselves have received from God." These women were living out God's word. What a revelation it was, too, when it was pointed out to me that we still had that baby. He or she would be waiting for us in heaven.

We soon began to feel that God was showing us that maybe He wanted us to be back in Ohio when we started our family. I truly longed to build a closer relationship with my mother. She had endured so much loss and heartache, and maybe the joys of being a grandmother would change her life. That would mean another new destination. God provided Linsey with a wonderful new job, and we moved once more. We bought another small farm for our dogs and now two horses.

I was scared, but we decided to try again for a baby. Finally, on June 10, 1982, Joshua Grant Borders was born, by caesarean section, at almost ten pounds. It was a smooth, noneventful pregnancy, although I was a nervous wreck from start to finish. He was quite a big bundle of joy! He was the most beautiful thing I had ever seen. He was such a happy, good baby. He slept through the night by the age of three months. His smiles could melt any heart and he brought more happiness and laughter to us than we could have ever imagined. My mother was overjoyed, and I could hardly recognize the love and affection that oozed out of her in this new role. Mom and I were finally finding some common ground. There were never any apologies or deep heart-to-heart talks between us, but there were many precious times of laughter and happiness, centered around Josh, and later, Jeremy. I couldn't have asked for a better grandmother for our sons. "And we know that in all things God works for the good of those who love him, who have been called according to his purpose," Romans 8:28.

Not long after Josh's first birthday, we were thinking that maybe we'd like to add baby number two, and I realized that I was pregnant already. All was going perfectly until I was six months along and discovered that I had a life-threatening condition to both myself and our baby, called Placenta Previa. I ended up in the hospital, flat on my back for five weeks. Linsey and Josh moved in with my very best friend and her busy family, who lived much closer to the hospital. She took care of Josh while Linsey worked. She'd come visit me and listen to me rant about being stuck in bed, going stir crazy. It was so great to have her back in my life. The drugs they gave me caused me to lash out with fits of anger and temper tantrums. I even hallucinated once. It was so scary.

After two blood transfusions, some critical moments and yet another cesarean section, Jeremy Ray Borders came into the world in a hurry. He was eight weeks premature. He also came in a big package, at seven pounds and one ounce. The doctors assured us that he was a preemie on the inside. We would learn later that Jeremy only operated in one speed, that being "Mach three with his hair on fire." Wow! We were now a family of four. My mother was thrilled to be Nana to two boys, and we were all happy and doing really well. Our desire was to stay right there on our peaceful little farm, raise our family, and serve the Lord.

Chapter Eight

L insey came home from work one day with shocking news. He'd lost his job. We had no indication that this was about to happen. He was a Corporate Safety Supervisor at a large national company and had recently been promoted to Corporate Manager of Human Resources. He loved his job but it required him to travel all over the United States and Canada. There were months, before the children were born, when he'd be gone for almost three weeks at a time. He'd been placed on a fast track to success, a young man amidst many senior executives with decades more experience. The company politics strangled him.

The day he was fired I remember bowing my head and thanking the Lord that, at least at that point in our life, we'd been walking with Him long enough and closely enough to know that God was in charge, and somehow good would come out of it. By now I had a few trials under my belt, and I was starting to understand that the Lord uses trials to strengthen us, to build our faith and to point us toward our next destination. It's not a ride in the park at the time and it's never something we willingly sign up for, but it's how God operates. "For my thoughts are not your thoughts, neither are your ways my ways, declares the Lord," Isaiah 58:8. It's up to us to trust, obey and yield. Thankfully, Linsey had no problem finding another suitable job. Good did come out of it. It meant more following Jesus to a completely new place, Columbia, South Carolina.

Chapter Nine

Another move! How would the folks down South take to the "transplanted Yankees" we were about to become? Well, they embraced us with open arms. South Carolina became our home for the next twenty years.

We joyfully adopted y'all, sweet tea, grits, humidity, heat, and the love of sand between our toes, as easily as if we'd been born down there.

We decided to part with our beloved horses before our move South. I knew I was a confirmed horse addict. When I was with the boys I wanted to be riding. When I was riding I felt I needed to be with my boys. God had been so good to give me horses, but He had also been so good to allow me to become a mom, and that hadn't come easily. I took my new calling very seriously. I knew I'd never be the mom that He wanted me to be if I kept the horses. We were able to find them amazing homes, and we said our goodbyes, not knowing if this was for forever, or not.

Linsey continued in the same line of work, including travel, but his trips were not as far away or as often. He had many business appointments in Myrtle Beach. During the years before the boys were in school, we were all able to tag along on those trips. We'd stay in a nice hotel with an indoor pool and the boys and I would swim and play all day until Linsey came home, and then we'd go out for dinner and enjoy more amusements along the "Grand Strand" during the evenings. We reminded the boys often, of how blessed we were to have this lifestyle. Many families saved up all year for a week at the beach and we were able to enjoy these trips at least once a month, year round.

We found the perfect neighborhood in the Columbia, South Carolina area. Each home had about an acre of land, and there were many young families with children around the same ages as ours, living close by. There were plenty of other stay-at-home moms around, and there was even a weekly Bible study group that met at our neighbor's house right up the street.

We had an in-ground pool, so our home became the "place to be" in the summer months. We loved that, because we were always there to supervise and get to know the kids and their families.

Linsey coached many of the boys' sports. Josh, especially, loved basketball, soccer and softball. Jeremy was in gymnastics for a few years until the meets began to require us to be out of town on Sundays. After a solemn discussion about how this would affect the future of our family and our relationship to being a part of our church, it was decided, and completely agreed upon by Jeremy, that this was not the path we should follow.

Soon Jeremy began taking piano lessons. Although not a sport, he learned that there was such a thing as competitive piano. He was gifted and he excelled in the competitions, usually winning at the state level each year in his age group, which allowed him to be part of a PBS television program that featured all the winners annually. Musical talent was something we all enjoyed. I was self-taught at guitar and song writing and enjoyed singing and playing at church. Linsey loved being in the choir and occasionally in a men's quartet. Joshua began playing guitar when he was in middle school, and it was clear that he had a God-given gift as well, both in playing and song-writing. Life was good.

Chapter Ten

A t this point, we had now made twelve moves within four states. I wondered if we had Gypsy blood! God was teaching me so many things. He seemed to be giving each new locale a "theme," as if in chapters of a book. That first "chapter," back in South Bend, Indiana, seemed to be on the subject of faithfulness. As a new Christian I needed to learn to be faithful, to reading my Bible, praying and going to church. I needed to restructure my life in order to develop godly habits that could help me grow. Lord knows, I'd not been successful structuring my life, my way. So many people today place no importance on attending church. With the internet, podcasts and online ministries, it's easy to discount the need to actually show up in a physical building, on Sunday mornings. In Hebrews 10:25 it says "Not giving up meeting together, as some are in the habit of doing, but encouraging one another." We need the fellowship.We need to be there to hear about the needs of others so we can pray, help, share meals and celebrate our joys and sorrows together. When I had my miscarriage, how would I have been encouraged, as a brand new believer, if all the ladies who reached out to me had only been "watching church" online? I would have been alone in my sorrow and confusion. We need each other. God designed us that way.

There was another "chapter" on giving, with a joyful heart. I learned that we cannot out give God. It all belongs to Him to start with. He has given us so much and He needs us to give back, with our money, and time spent in serving. Malachi 3:10 says "Bring the whole tithe into the storehouse, that there may be food in my house. Test me in this, says the Lord Almighty, and see if I will not throw open the floodgates of heaven and pour out so much blessing that there will not be room enough to store it." Put Him to the test. Give and it will be given unto you.

Praise and Worship. This was one of the most beautiful chapters in my life from the Lord. A whole new world opened up to me in the realm of listening to, playing and singing Christian music. I had no idea of the variety of genres that existed under the heading "Christian" and it was exciting to explore them all. It was so fulfilling to be able to praise Him for this whole new person I was becoming. I was never more filled with joy than when I was praising the Lord, lifting my hands, and feeling His presence in ways I had never felt before.

Even with these beautiful chapters in my life, I still had so much growing to do. Some of my dearest friends and loved ones were going through tough times. I wanted to be there for them. I wanted to have a shoulder for them to cry on, and offer a sincere, listening ear. Too often though, my world revolved only around me and my family. I was a busy mom and I didn't have much time for others, or was it an intentional choice on my part? Was I void of compassion? I'd had a few bumps along the way in my life, but things usually turned out pretty well for me in the end. Maybe I could not relate to folks who were hurting. So I began to pray. I asked God if He would make me more of a blessing to others, because I didn't feel like I was much of one at all.

God began to answer that prayer in a way that I would have never imagined. As I began to see the next journey that He was expecting me to take, He gave me the following words to another song:

YOU'VE GOT THE ARMOR

by Vicki Borders
1992

I woke up one morning, my heart sank to the floor. The trial I feared the most in life was camped outside my door.
I cried and cried all day, I couldn't even pray, except to ask the Lord, "How could you treat your child this way?"
The days they slowly turned to weeks, and I allowed the Lord to speak, "My child, you're not forsaken, though you're helpless now and weak
You've stood for Me in good times, will you stand for Me in bad? It hurts, but you must face this toughest trial you've ever had."

You've got the armor, the helmet and the sword; that's My salvation, and My living word
Be girded with the Truth, and wear your shoes of peace, hold tightly to your shield of faith, till Satan's darts do cease.

So many more are dying, so many yet are lost; I need to know who'll do My will, no matter what the cost
And don't forget that roaring lion, who waits at every turn; he'll never win if you put on your armor, and stand firm.

I'll wake up some sunny day, when this old world has passed
away and all those scars and trials
will seem so old and far away, and I'll hang up my armor, and
sit down by His throne
And sing an endless song of praise to Him who led me home.

You've got the armor, the helmet and the sword; that's My salvation, and My living word
Be girded with the Truth, and wear your shoes of peace, hold
tightly to your shield of faith till Satan's darts do cease.

Chapter Eleven

I truly did wake up one morning and I found that my life would never again be the same. Job 3:25 says "What I feared has come upon me; what I dreaded has happened to me." I did have this one great fear in my life. I'd harbored it for many years. I'd talked to the Lord about it so many times that I truly believed that, because I was His child, if I honored and worshipped and served and loved Him enough, that He might spare me from this one great fear in my life. All the loving and honoring, serving and worshipping was real and from my heart, but God didn't choose to work that way. He wanted to show me that there was nothing in this life that I couldn't face, with Him by my side.

My favorite aunt died when she was in her fifties. You would have loved my Aunt Dot. She was the female version of Dr. Doolittle. She had a zest for life and a way with animals like no one I have ever known. She was a gentle lady, smiling to the very end. I spent a lot of time with her out at her farm while I was growing up. I know she contributed greatly to my intense love of animals. When she died, a part of me went with her.

A few years after her death, when I was in Washington DC, I got a call from my mother one day. She said she was about to face major surgery. She was facing the very same dilemma that had killed my aunt. She was wondering if I would come home to be with her and my younger sister while she was in the hospital.

Of course I came home, and I thanked the Lord that she came through the surgery just fine. I began to appraise this situation though... first my aunt and now my mom. Was she going to die too? This was getting awfully close to home, and awfully close to me. Even though I was a very young woman at the time, a real, permanent fear settled into my heart. I sensed that I, too, might have to face this one day.

Time passed. My aunt had been in her fifties when she died. My mother had been in her forties when this same trial came her way. Fast-forward to me. I was in my thirties. There are things in our lives that we never, ever forget, like our first date, our first kiss, our wedding day, the day our children were born and so many other unforgettable milestone moments. Well, you'll never forget what it's like when your doctor comes into your room and looks at you soberly and tells you that you have cancer. What? This really did happen? This had to be some cruel, horrible joke. I was in my thirties. I felt great. I thought I took good care of myself. What about Linsey and the boys? Jeremy was in the second grade and Josh was in the fourth. Was I going to die? I was a child of the King. This was not supposed to happen to me.

I remember telling Linsey one night, how I really felt. I shared that it was as if there was this loving father, who had a daughter who was terrified of vicious dogs. He decided that the only way he could teach her about those dogs was to turn one loose on her, and then stand in the background and call out "It's ok, I love you. It's for your good. You'll do fine." That's how scared and terrified I really was.

I quickly learned that this was a two-part chapter in my life, from the Lord. The subject of the first half was suffering.

Part two, though, was about the relevance of God's Word. Up until this point in my life, I was trying to make time to read the Bible. I could find most of the books contained therein. I had an array of favorite verses and a pretty good knowledge of most of the major events and stories. When this happened, however, I began to plunge myself into the Word, as a drowning man gasps for air. I learned more and more. I read from the Psalmist, for example, that it was ok to bite, kick and scream. He did! King David said this to the Lord in Psalm 6:5-6 "Among the dead no one proclaims your name. Who praises you from the grave? I am worn out from my groaning. All night long I flood my couch with tears." Those verses were for me and I read them over and over and pled to the Lord for mercy and for healing.

Soon, the Lord began to speak to my aching, trembling heart and He began to tell me that I could face the days ahead, because He would give me the strength that I needed. It was as if He was saying "It's ok, I am with you and you can do this." He was there with me in ways that were beyond describing. Those were tough days though. I faced bi-lateral mastectomies and reconstructive surgeries. There were days when I wondered if I'd ever want to face anyone ever again.

I came across a verse where the Lord said, in Hebrews 12:2, "For the joy set before Him, He endured the cross, scorning its shame." I began to think about the fact that Jesus did not enjoy the suffering He endured on that cross for you and me, but that it was out of a heart of pure love that He did it. I would have called upon ten thousand angels to come and rescue me from this horrible turn of events in my life, and Jesus certainly could have, but He said "proceed."

Another verse I found was Phillipians 3:10 (KJV), "That I may know Him and the power of His resurrection and the fellowship of His sufferings, being made conformable unto His death." I meditated on that term "the fellowship of His sufferings." I believe that it means that He sees it as a privilege when He chooses us to suffer. When we are laid low in a valley, we get a glimpse of our Savior that I don't think we can get at any other time, as to how He loved us so much that he volunteered to suffer, so that we could have eternal life and be with Him forever. Having cancer was not suffering for my faith; it was in no way comparable to being burned at the stake for refusing to deny the Lord, or being persecuted for Christ in a hostile ISIS imprisonment. For me, though, at that time, it was a degree of suffering that I had never experienced. It was something completely out of my control, unlike my Savior, who chose from the foundations of the earth that He would suffer unlike anyone has, or ever will, for us.

Chapter Twelve

Little by little, I began to recover from this huge ordeal in my life. Sure enough, the Lord began sending people across my path who were going through the same trials. I began to feel compassion. When I told someone I would pray for them, I really did. Too many times I used to say that I would pray for someone, but then forget.

I knew there had to be some new way that the Lord wanted me to serve Him. He had done so much for me that I could hardly contain myself. First, I became a volunteer for the American Cancer Society's "Reach for Recovery" program. To my surprise, I received a plaque for Volunteer of the Year at their annual banquet. I visited women, post surgery, to talk to them, encourage them, and give them tips on exercises and post breast cancer care. I rejoiced when they recovered and I mourned when some of them didn't. I loved serving those women, but I didn't feel as free to share my faith in Christ with them as I wanted.

In that setting, I was really brave. I was uncomfortable and embarrassed, though, to talk about any of this in any other setting. The Lord reminded me one day that I had pled to Him for mercy and healing and promised Him that if He would spare my life, I would gladly make known to others His great mercy and His willingness, even in our generation, to still perform miracles. He had healed me, but I had kept silent. As I healed and studied, prayed and meditated, more music and lyrics began to flow into me from the Lord on this subject.

WILL YOU ONLY SING TO THE NIGHT?

by Vicki Borders
1994

Today I reached for a handle, and before me a door opened wide
I looked into a room filled with wonderful treasures, all waiting
for me inside.
Then I asked the Lord, why the treasures were stored and not
already mine to keep
The answer He gave made me feel so ashamed that I fell down
and started to weep, started to weep.

How can they hear of Jesus, if you only sing to the night?
How can they envision the kingdom to come if you keep your
paint box closed tight?
How can they know the Good Shepherd will tenderly care for
their needs
If instead of going out to water and plant, you sit on your
sack of seeds?

It's true I praised Him from the shadows, too afraid to speak
out in the light
I shared just a hint of the feelings inside, I sang my best songs
to the night
So few have a clue of the miracles, that He has performed
just for me
Now He's opened a door, I can't wait anymore, I'll boldly speak
out as He leads, as He leads.

I will paint a bright picture with colors and words, showing
mercy and healing love

I will tend to His saplings and scatter new seed for the heavenly garden above

How can they hear of Jesus if we only sing to the night?
How can they envision the kingdom to come if we keep our paint box closed tight?
How can they know the Good Shepherd will tenderly care for their needs
If instead of going out to water and plant, we sit on our sack of seeds?
If instead of going out to water and plant, we sit on our sack of seeds.

Chapter Thirteen

G od was preparing me for a radically new destination.
I signed up for a song-writing course at Columbia International University in Columbia, South Carolina. I had written several other new songs during my recovery period. I was beginning to have a strong desire to share them, along with all that I was learning from God through this. It was our pastor who suggested that I take this class. I had been working for him as a part-time church secretary. He was not just my boss, but a special friend, like a brother I never had. He enjoyed my music and told me that he had been praying for a long time that I would do more with it.

It turned out that this class not only taught song writing, but was a tutorial on music ministry and how to, with God's direction, get started. It began to be clear to me that this was where God was leading. The Lord had reached His hand down from heaven and touched my body and allowed it to be healed, and He had touched my soul and allowed me to understand that I had eternal life. I wanted to share this with anyone who would listen. Soon, "HIS LAMB I AM" ministry was born, named after a song I wrote with that same title:

HIS LAMB I AM

by Vicki Borders
1994

His lamb I am, He turned and left the fold, to rescue me when I was wandering, lost and cold
His lamb I am, He rules the earth and sky, but somehow He has time to wipe each tear I cry
He paid the awful price, His own blood sacrifice, to make me part of His great plan,
His lamb I am.

His lamb I am, my blessings overflow, my Shepherd whispers to me everywhere I go
His lamb I am, He raised me new and strong, He gave me hope, put in my heart a brand new song.
No sword or power unseen, can tear His eyes off me, or pull me from His loving hand,
His lamb I am.

His lamb I am, I long to see His face, and thank Him for His mercy and His wondrous grace
His lamb I am, I'll serve Him to the end, for never have I felt such love from any friend
No sword or power unseen, can tear His eyes off me, or pull me from His loving hand, His lamb I am, His lamb I am, His lamb I am.

Our pastor allowed me to share my first one-hour program with our own congregation. Many friends from the community came as well, and two people began a brand new relationship with

Jesus Christ that evening. I was elated! God had used it. Soon our family was on the road, wherever God would open a door, visiting other churches, large and small, to share my music and testimony. Linsey would run the sound system and the boys were the roadies. It was a family affair that I hope and pray made a difference to our sons and helped shape their service to the Lord today.

Chapter Fourteen

A t one of the churches where we ministered, I met a woman who was a well-known Christian singer, who also traveled and shared her own testimony. She and her husband had been in an auto accident and she had suffered from amnesia for almost a year, and the Lord miraculously brought her through it. After she heard my concert, she offered to help me. I was a bit "star-struck" at first, because I had heard her songs on the radio and I had such admiration for her. It was through her that I learned about a national organization called Stonecroft Ministries, established in 1938. She told me that what I did would really fit very well into their format. When her schedule permitted, she spoke and sang for Stonecroft events and she invited me to go with her to her next engagement.

I was immediately impressed by this ministry. The meetings, called Womens' Connections, are held in country clubs or banquet rooms in restaurants and hotels. They provide a luncheon or dinner and a program that is of interest to women, such as a fashion show, make-up demonstration or a trendy business idea. They usually invite a soloist, and then at the end of the affair, a speaker comes and shares her life story, including how she came to accept Jesus Christ as her personal Savior. She then invites the women to accept Christ by prayer, and to fill out a confidential card which is turned in to the local club. The club then follows up with those women, and they are invited to prayer coffees and Bible studies, and are encouraged to join local churches. I felt that this would be the perfect fit for my ministry. I knew I would be more comfortable sharing my testimony with other women and the opportunities to speak were plentiful. I could be as busy as I wanted, and not interfere with Linsey's job or our family time. My talk was approved by Stonecroft and for the next ten years, I traveled, spoke and shared my songs with many wonderful women. I began in South Carolina, but I also spoke in North Carolina, Georgia, Virginia and Florida, West Virginia and Ohio. God allowed me to point hundreds to Christ and I made lifelong, eternal friendships through this experience.

Chapter Fifteen

After eight years in our neighborhood in the Columbia area, several families we were closest to had moved away, due to job transfers. A lot had changed, and Linsey decided that the Charleston, South Carolina area would be a better location for him to work. He worked out of our home, but still did extensive travel all around the state and this would save hours of driving. We were packing up again. I sure wish we would have bought stock in a moving company!

We were off to beautiful, historic Charleston, South Carolina, nicknamed the "Holy City." City ordinances there state that no building can be built taller than the tallest church steeple, and there are many historic churches scattered throughout the downtown area.

We were excited to be closer to the beach too. With the boys both in school and involved in so many activities, we no longer accompanied Linsey to Myrtle Beach very often. It would be great to be only minutes away from the beautiful ocean. It turned out that our church's youth pastor lived right next door to our new home. The boys loved his leadership and the church had a great youth group. Our lives were filled with sports, music, church activities and fun in the sun.

I continued to travel and speak for Stonecroft. I loved this calling, and I was sad to see that there was not a Christian

Women's Club in the Charleston area. As I visited the other clubs, I could see the close friendships and relationships that were fostered, but, for me, it was always good-bye, and then I was on my way to my next engagement. I longed to see a local club emerge so that I could experience that same camaraderie and outreach. I contacted Stonecroft to learn how to go about doing that. It was a long, arduous process, not without our enemy, the devil, trying to dig his fingers into it, with heartache and drama, to try to kill it before it ever got off the ground. God was faithful though, and it succeeded.

In January of 2000, the Berkeley County Christian Women's Club was birthed. I was able to serve as the first Chairwoman. We met at the beautiful Oaks Country Club and, true to my hopes and prayers, we served many wonderful women, pointing them to our Lord Jesus Christ, and seeing their lives change in so many ways. I made close friendships that I still hold near and dear today.

God has a plan for each of us! He wants us to go out and share His love with others. There is such a shortage of that going on today. We need to take the time to share what the Lord is doing in our lives, whether it's in a formal setting or just across the table, over a cup of coffee or at lunch with an unsaved friend. We all need to have relationships with those who need the Lord. We can't live in a bubble, surrounded only by those who name the name of Christ. It's up to us to be His hands, His feet and His voice. As long as we have life and breath, we are never too young or too old.

Chapter Sixteen

H ow time flies. In the blink of an eye the boys were already in high school. Years earlier, our niece, Laurel, had come to South Carolina to live with us, and had become like a big sister to Josh and Jeremy, and like a daughter to us. She first came down for one summer to help me the year I was recovering from my cancer surgeries. When she went back to Ohio for her senior year of high school, she was headed for serious trouble. Her mom, Linsey's sister, asked us if we would consider having her come back to live with us for awhile after graduation. She saw what an influence we'd previously been on her and how close we had become. She was truly worried. We were happy to have her back. We set down some strict guidelines and told her that she would be heading right back home with the first broken rule. Zero tolerance. There was only ever one small confrontation, and she cried and begged for forgiveness. We quickly forgave her and soon she began a personal relationship with Christ while living with us. Her life changed dramatically. Her testimony was an inspiration to our family and to everyone who knew her. After staying with us for over a year, she was accepted to attend Liberty University in Lynchburg, Virginia. It was there that, in addition to receiving a great education, she met a wonderful, godly Christian man who became her husband.

We loved to visit Laurel at college, which was when Josh decided that he'd like to attend there too. He was a good student and had been able to take college courses while in high school, so he was in good shape even before starting. He auditioned for one of the colleges' traveling praise bands, and was accepted. While going to school, he'd be traveling to many exciting places to sing, play guitar, and share Christ.

Six weeks to the day before the tragedy of 9/11, he and the band from Liberty University were standing on the top of the World Trade Center in New York City. They'd been in the area, singing and serving. What a chilling reality it was for us to realize that had the tragedy occurred only six weeks earlier, Josh would have perished. We were so proud of him and so thankful for God's grace.

When Josh left for college, Jeremy was about to begin his junior year of high school. Jeremy continued to be heavily involved in studying classical piano. He was winning many competitions. The summer before his junior year, he won the Junior Brevard Music competition and was invited to attend a summer music camp in Asheville, North Carolina. At the end of the camp, after a special presentation by all the students, it was announced that those who had performed that day had been invited to attend the South Carolina Governor's School for the Arts, in Greenville, South Carolina, beginning that fall. This was a two year residential program, where the students would be given highly specialized training in their field of the arts, in addition to finishing high school. At that time the tuition was paid for by the state of South Carolina, and the facilities were brand new and beautiful. How could we refuse him this opportunity? It was such an honor. It meant, however, that we would be saying goodbye to not one, but to BOTH of our sons at the same time.

We were sad that the time had passed so quickly, but we were prepared for Josh to be heading off to Virginia. We expected to have Jeremy home for another two years.

I was devastated. This was the end of an era for me. I was the one who never cared about being a mom. I just wanted to be involved in all things "four-legged." I waited a long time, and when I experienced motherhood, I was filled with more joy than I'd ever imagined, raising and loving those two boys. Now I felt like I was being fired from the greatest job I'd ever had. These were amazing new destinations for our sons, but not for me. I cried and mourned for much of the first year they were gone. If it hadn't been for my husband, my speaking engagements, and our local chapter of the Christian Women's Club, I don't know how I would have survived.

Time is a healer, though, and I did survive. Eventually, Josh did an internship with FOX News in Charleston, while still at Liberty. They liked him so much that upon graduation, in December 2003, he was hired as a photo journalist and came back home, although not for long. He'd had a professor at Liberty who was with ABC News, who really liked Josh and remembered him when an opening came available at the Lynchburg affiliate. Josh had made close friendships in Lynchburg and liked the idea of returning, so he soon moved back to Virginia.

Once he was back in Lynchburg, Josh started a blues/rock band called Hot Like Cajun. The guys had all been college friends. He wrote all of their music and they gathered quite a following, packing out several clubs and restaurants in the area, on a regular basis. They recorded three cds, had their faces on billboards around Lynchburg for awhile, and played at a national JeepFest. We loved to get out and hear them. After all, we did meet on a dance floor! To this day, whenever our parrot (we've had Captain Crunch, a Goffin's Cockatoo, for twenty-seven years so far) hears one of Josh's songs playing, he goes nuts, rocking out to the music.

After Jeremy graduated from the SC Governor's School, he received a scholarship from the University of Houston's Moore's School of Music, where he majored in Piano Performance and Composition. He stayed in Texas after graduation and went to work teaching piano at a private school of the arts. He also did private concerts, played for corporate functions and did anything "musical" that opened up for him. He loved big city life and seemed to be very happy.

Chapter Seventeen

T he week of our thirtieth wedding anniversary, we took a trip to Lynchburg to see Josh and Laurel and her family. We had a great visit. We had just bought a brand new truck. We'd only owned it ten days. After going out to breakfast and saying our goodbyes, we headed back to South Carolina.

On the way home, I was perusing through my Bible and I read the 25th Psalm out loud. The writer asked God to lift us up, not let our enemies triumph over us and to help us not to be ashamed before Him. It speaks of God's lovingkindness, His forgiveness and His ability to pluck us out of the net that our enemies would have us fall into. I was feeling so at peace.

We drove a couple hours and then Linsey asked me if we could switch drivers. We were traveling a different route than usual. It was a four-lane highway with a grass median, and a sixty-five mph speed limit. I was driving along in the right lane and I saw a semi truck about to merge. I had just turned on the headlights because it was overcast. I signaled and got into the left lane to allow the trucker to enter the highway. We were about halfway past the truck as he merged onto the road, when we nervously observed that he was coming right on over into our lane. Our truck was just behind the back of his cab at that point. I decided to speed up a little, thinking he would surely see us, but he kept on coming. By now I had two tires on the grass median. He kept on coming. In a split second, I was completely on the grass and out of harm's way, but the grass was wet and our cruise control was on. When we hit the grass, the rear end of the truck began to swing around, and we were flying sideways down a slight incline toward the steel-cable guard rail in the middle of the median. In my terror, Linsey said that I had stomped on the gas instead of the brake. We smashed the metal cable and took off with a new fury, fishtailing and spinning around in the wet grass, continuing down the median.

My life was passing before my eyes. I wasn't aware of Linsey even being beside me. I wasn't thinking of Josh or Jeremy or anyone. On the inside, I felt almost suspended in mid-air, strangely aware of a "battle" going on. I don't know what prevented us from rolling over. The next thing I remembered, was that we made one final surge back up onto the road. I knew that this had to be "it." As the tires hit the pavement, I slammed on the brakes and we came to a stop in the left lane of the highway, FACE TO FACE with the same semi that had run us off the road. He had finally spotted us after we hit the median and he was slowing down during our entire ordeal. He was able to get his rig stopped only one car length between us. When I looked up, at the same moment that I realized we were still alive, I saw another car across the highway go flying across the median, through the cables and come to a stop. Our accident had caused a second accident on the other side. I was hysterical, not with fear, but with joy and amazement that God had supernaturally protected us and we had no major injuries.

After being detained nearly two hours at the scene, we were finally on our way home. I was quiet, lost in my thoughts. Linsey asked me if I realized that I had screamed the name of Jesus five or six times while we were swerving and spinning. A flood of tears came! What Linsey didn't know, was that over the past few months, I had prayed to grow even closer to my Lord. I told Him that I feared that if I was ever confronted with a life or death situation, that I would think of everyone but Him. I wondered if His name would enter my thoughts or cross my lips. I wanted Him to be the only one on my mind in such a situation. I don't remember saying a single word during those terror-filled seconds, but I am so relieved to know that Jesus was there and that I was screaming out to Him, on "auto-pilot." Romans 8:26 says that "the Spirit helps us in our weakness. We do not know what we ought to pray for, but the Spirit Himself intercedes for us with groans that words cannot express." Wow! Thank you, Lord. Years later, I still shiver when we get close to big semi trucks on the highway.

Chapter Eighteen

Now that we were empty nesters, memories of my years spent with horses began to seep back into my heart and mind. I was still speaking and involved with our Christian Women's Club, but there was an empty spot in my heart that was always reserved for my love of all things equine. I found a lady who rescued former race horses, who agreed to allow me to come and exercise them once in a while. This was like giving a drink to an alcoholic. I told Linsey that this might not be a good idea, because having a "taste of the tortilla" would make me want the whole enchilada. I was right. I soon wanted to own my very own horse again.

During this time we had begun attending a different church in Summerville, South Carolina. What a unique ministry they had. This church was given a gorgeous horse farm to manage and use. I had never heard of such a thing. The farm had a large, beautiful repurposed barn that the church used for retreats and gatherings. A young couple lived in a caretakers' house there and cared for their own, and a few privately-owned horses that were not used by the church, except to provide a beautiful back-drop and ambience, whenever people gathered.

Josh's former girlfriend's mother was a horse owner. We stayed friends long after their break-up, due to our common love of the Lord and horses. We also attended the same church.

One Sunday, she approached me with some information about a mare that was for sale. Her friend was having health problems and she had to downsize her herd of beloved Arabians. One of the horses had already been moved to a nearby stable in hopes of finding just the right home. Was I interested? I'd been praying and I was waiting on the Lord. Linsey had given me his blessing and I was so excited I could hardly sleep at night. I wanted to find the horse that God had picked out for me. He owns the cattle on a thousand hills, the Bible says, so He would have just the right horse for me.

We went to meet this horse that our friend had told us about and soon "Sapphire" became mine. What a beauty. My first and second horses were Morgans. I like to think of that breed as the "teddy bears" of the horse world. I had never owned an Arabian. I now think of them as the "French Poodles" of the horse world. Sapphire was still young and at times, she could be so unpredictable. We could ride past a bush or an ant hill five times with no reaction, and then on the sixth time, she would decide it was a fire-breathing dragon, bent on eating her for lunch. Once, she even dragged me, after a large Pampas Grass bush gave her the wrong look. Needless to say, my riding skills improved quickly, for my own self-preservation.

We boarded Sapphire at the church farm. It was such a beautiful place and beside it was a private hunt club with acres of trails to ride on. Before long, my dear husband decided that he would like to buy a horse too. I was a little surprised. In the early years when we'd owned our first farm, Linsey had no desire to ride. He loved being around the horses, but not on them. There was "that time" when he tried riding Captain and Captain stopped short of the fence line, but Linsey didn't. There was also "that time" when Linsey tried to mount, bareback, and he somehow ended up on the other side of the horse, on the ground. Enough said. We now had some really nice trails to ride, though, and that appealed to him, so he was wanting to give it another try.

Soon we found "Rocky," a handsome Quarter Horse gelding. We jokingly called him "Rachmaninhoof" because Jeremy had been learning concertos by the great Russian composer, Rachmaninoff, and that was all he was talking about. What fun it was to be able to trail ride together. We spent hours of our free time out at the farm.

Our pastor spent some of his free time out at the farm on his "horse" too. His steed was a big riding mower. He loved to spend time mowing, praying and meditating there. He had rented a suit of armor and a horse when he proposed to his wife. Evidently, the horse didn't appreciate the clanging metal suit, and our dear pastor ended up proposing from the ground, and not from the saddle. He said that the only horse he'd ever ride again would be his trusty John Deere. I probably would have never gotten to know him, had it not been for his love of mowing.

The Lord began to impress upon him the fact that horses could be used for a lot more at this farm than just as beautiful scenery. He approached me one day, knowing I was a church member and a horse-addict, and asked if I would pray about ways that we could implement the use of the horses there, for the benefit of the Lord.

Chapter Nineteen

G od is so good. "But seek first His kingdom and His righteousness, and all these things will be given to you as well," Matthew 6:33. There it was again. I had always had a secret desire, on my "list of things," if you will, to work with horses in a much bigger way. I began to do some research on horse ministry and I was so impressed with what people were doing with them to reach others for Christ.

The first thing I proposed was that we begin an affordable riding lesson program. When I was a kid, I would have given my eye teeth to have been able to take riding lessons. They were always so expensive, so that left me as the young girl who leaned against the outside of the fence and watched, longingly, as other kids rode. When I finally took lessons as an adult, my instructor was so harsh, that at times, I came home crying. I had made a mental note back then, that if I were ever given the chance to teach, I would do things differently. My proposal was given the green light. I was elated! Linsey and I found a few school horses, which the church purchased, and we appealed to other local horse operations to donate to our cause. We received helmets, saddles, and a myriad of other items that we needed for the program. One weekend, the youth group came out and painted and fixed up the tack room so we could have everything clean and organized. We were ready to go.

The church had a good number of home school families who eagerly signed their kids up for lessons. They were available during daytime, weekday hours which worked out so well. What fun we had. My classes were purposely small, so I could give each child individual attention and keep them really safe. I incorporated fun and games into my lessons and I shared "horsey-themed" Bible truths with my students at each lesson, such as this one: Consider the salt block. This is a heavy, white cube which horses love to lick. It provides them with salt and minerals, and makes them thirsty so they drink plenty of water. The Bible says in Matthew 5:13, "You are the salt of the earth." We need to tell others about Jesus. By doing that, we provide them with God's love and we make them thirsty for a relationship with the Lord.

I also made small, laminated "Canter Club" cards for my students. Once they could walk, trot and canter their horses by themselves with control and safety, they became a member of my Canter Club. The card was printed with the verse from Isaiah 40:31(KJV), which says "They that wait upon the Lord shall renew their strength; they shall "MOUNT UP"(my emphasis) with wings of eagles; they shall "RUN" and not be weary; they shall "WALK" and not faint." It was a little play on God's Word, and we made a big deal of presenting the card to the kids when they earned it, and they proudly carried their cards around. I met up with one of my former students, all grown up, and she told me she still had her Canter Club card.

Another family that signed up was a father/son team. The whole family came out to watch each lesson and they often brought along a picnic lunch for me to enjoy with them after we were finished. I ended up teaching two more of their children and we became lifelong friends. God was blessing the program so much that soon I had a waiting list for this program.

For the next two summers, we also instituted day camps. The church members had many other great talents and activities to offer the kids besides the horses, such as basketball, canoeing, games, crafts, drama, Bible study and even a clown ministry. We teamed up with an inner-city church in Charleston for one of the camps and we also reached out to underprivileged and foster kids. What a great success these camps were. Many children learned about the love of Jesus Christ and invited Him into their lives.

Chapter Twenty

I was still speaking whenever I could and I remained blissfully in "horse heaven." I was working hard and constantly thinking of new ideas to improve our church's horse ministry. Linsey, however, was beginning to agonize over his job. He'd survived many corporate down-sizes with this current employer. His company had been bought out twice, and people were being asked to leave, one after another. He was sure he saw the writing on the wall.

He heard about a solid company out of Richmond, Virginia that also had operations in South Carolina. Soon he was being considered for a local position with that company. This was wonderful, because he would have job security and we could stay right where we were. As the interviewing process continued, however, Linsey learned that the company decided not to create the new position they had spoken of, in South Carolina. They had a position they really wanted him for, but this one was in central Virginia. There was no pay cut involved, the benefits were outstanding, and they were willing, not only to pay for our complete move, but to ship our horses as well. On paper, it was a no-brainer, but oh, NO, Lord! Why now, when our life was going so well and I felt I was being used like never before? It didn't make sense at all. The decision was soon made, though. I had to support my loving husband and our future. We were going to leave South Carolina after almost twenty years. I was devastated. I was inconsolable. I had truly believed that our moving days were over.

We made a trip to Virginia to look at properties. My request now was, that if we were going to move, could we please have our own farm again? It had been so many years since we'd owned acreage. We looked at quite a few properties and hiked through many pastures, trails and woods, trying to envision ourselves anew. There was one farm that made my heart do a "pitter-patter," but I realized that it was out of our price range, and I was sorry that we'd even looked at it.

We came home covered with chigger bites. We wanted to scratch our skin off. In all the years we'd been in South Carolina, we'd never been attacked by chiggers (aka red bugs/ demons from hell) and I'd only had one or two tick bites, ever. What kind of a bug-infested jungle were we going to move to? Surely this was a BAD detour.

I continued asking the Lord why He was moving us, and whether or not He really knew what He was doing. We listed our home the evening we got back. Within a few hours, our realtor called us and said he had two couples who wanted to see the house the next morning. We were shocked and hardly ready, but we consented. Low and behold, the first couple that showed up not only bought the property, but rounded the asking price UP to an even number. We sold our home in less than twenty-four hours! "Ok Lord," I said. "I get it. You are speaking loud and clear. We'll go get boxes. We'll call the movers. I'll start packing."

There was also the matter of King. King was a beautiful horse that we had found for the church riding lesson program. He had eyes that looked right into your soul and he became the favorite mount of so many of my students, and me as well. We bonded immediately and I could not imagine life without him. I told Linsey that I desperately needed this horse to go with us, in order for me to have total peace about the move. I knew this could be a challenge because King was so loved, but I cried and prayed to the Lord about it.

After we broke the sad news to the church and farm staff, I poured out my heart to them, concerning King. They said that if we could find a suitable replacement for him, King could become a Virginian. Just as we were leaving the farm office, one of the gals who fed the horses approached us and asked if we were aware that a new mare had arrived at the farm for private boarding. She was owned by a woman who was going through a painful divorce. She had been a former school horse, and she was for sale. Coincidence? I don't think so. That is the grace of our God. We were able to buy "Darcy" for the program and King was officially mine.

That same week the mother of our farm manager passed away. She was a beautiful, godly lady. At her funeral, someone read one of her favorite scriptures from her Bible. It was Isaiah 55:12. It says "You will go out in joy and be led forth in peace; the mountains and hills will burst into song before you, and all the trees of the field will clap their hands." When I heard that verse, my eyes filled with tears and I could hardly breathe. I didn't normally react like that. The Lord had just given me a verse to journey with. That verse has remained a special gift, personally handed to me from God, ever since that moment. I will always relate those words, and the peace they give me, to the beautiful Blueridge Mountains of Central Virginia.

Chapter Twenty-One

A fter a tearful cookout and farewell party attended by most of my students, their families, our pastor, and the farm staff, we headed North, toward those gorgeous mountains, with Sapphire, Rocky and King. We followed the horse hauler to be sure our precious cargo traveled safely. Would you believe, that before we even arrived in Virginia, the driver tried to buy King right off the trailer? He was quite a boy. He lived on our farm for twelve more years, died at a very old age, and is buried under a Chestnut tree in the back pasture. I have a heart necklace made of braided hair from his tail, which hangs on our rear view mirror. There are good animals, and there are great ones. He was one of the greatest. I'm sure I will see him again one day, along with all of our other beloved animals, who have crossed over that "rainbow bridge."

Would you also believe that God gave us that farm that made my heart skip a beat? How could I argue with God. He had flung open every door with this move and made His will so obvious that there was no denying that we were completely and totally supposed to be in Virginia. Between the time we first looked, and the time we returned, the sellers dropped the price of our "dream farm" to a level we could afford. I was still very sad to leave South Carolina and all of our dear friends and the ministries that I loved, but I was "over the moon" to be living on our very own farm again. I was now able to feed and care for our horses myself, and see them every day. Our home sat way back off the road. We had gorgeous views and total privacy. The land was quite level, which was hard to find in this part of Virginia, and the house was roomy and beautiful.

We hit the ground running. There was no barn and very little fencing. We boarded the horses for eight weeks until we could put up enough temporary fencing to keep them safe and contained. Linsey would work his day job and then get home and work for hours, building our new barn. My husband is so talented. I never dreamed he would be able to build such a beautiful structure with pretty much his own two hands and God's supernatural protection. I remember many times, seeing him balancing huge beams with ropes, pulleys and his trusty tractor, trying to set them in the ground. I would pray fervently for God to protect him from injury.

It was so much work, and at times we cried from stress and exhaustion, but it was such a gift to be able to map out the placement of the buildings, fencing and two riding arenas to our exact specifications. It was a monumental labor of love. When we left South Carolina, our pastor said that they now considered us a Virginia extension of the church's horse ministry, and that prayers for God's blessings and direction would be with us always. We surely could feel those prayers.

I learned that there was a chapter of Christian Women's Club in Central Virginia, but it was over an hour away. I attended the club for a short while and even spoke and sang there once. Praise the Lord, seven women desired to begin a relationship with Jesus that day. It wasn't a fit for me anymore, though. I didn't feel peace about being a part of the group. We were so busy building our farm, that I finally believed that God wanted me to put all my efforts into serving Him with the horses, and that it was ok to say goodbye to that part of my life. A dear friend told me she thought that one of the reasons God gave us that great farm and horse ministry was because of all the years I so unselfishly traveled and poured out my heart to those many dear women.

We arrived in Virginia in August, 2004. By spring of the following year, I signed up my first riding students and the "Full Circle Farm" Ministry was born. We named the farm "Full Circle." It had such meaning to us. I lived in Falls Church, Virginia and worked in Langley, when I met Linsey. He proposed to me in Reston, Virginia, when bumper stickers with "Virginia is for Lovers" abounded. Linsey wasn't born in Virginia, but he was born in the mountains of West Virginia, and now he was returning to a backdrop of mountains, which he'd missed for many years. We were also back on our own farm, since that first little farm we owned in Ohio. We were going to be back in horse ministry too. I'm skipping ahead a bit, but my very first horse was a Morgan horse. We soon found the sweetest twin Morgan geldings for our riding program. The Lord blessed us double. It seemed like everywhere we looked we saw another full circle.

Less than six months after we arrived in Virginia, we shockingly learned that our church in South Carolina had made the decision to end their relationship with the horse farm. The owner was going to sell and it was decided that there were many more pressing ministry issues for the future of the church, than being involved with a farm. I could hardly believe it. God knew that this would be happening and He moved us to Virginia so we could continue with what He'd planned for us to do in South Carolina. How devastating it would have been, had we stayed and had to watch it all be pulled out from under us. We were soon contacted and asked if we wanted any of the saddles, equipment and even one of the horses for our new ministry. We happily made a trip back and arrived home with "Blaze," a sweet school horse that we had found for the church, and also a load of stuff that we desperately needed. Our cup was running over. God was showing up and showing off on a daily basis. We had to pinch ourselves to believe that we weren't dreaming.

Soon, more kids were signing up and I was back in my element, teaching, building relationships with the students and their families, and sharing the love of the Lord Jesus Christ at each appointed lesson. Remember the dear family in South Carolina who signed up for lessons and brought the picnics? They came up for a visit in the spring and helped us clear a riding trail through the woods. Someone from our new church came out with some heavy equipment and helped with the trail too. He said that because it was for a ministry, there would be no charge. We now had a mile-long loop trail through the woods to enjoy. The Canter Club was back in effect and now when my students mastered their tasks, I allowed them to go on a guided trail ride. During the winter, I painted wooden signs with the words to appropriate Bible verses which we tacked on trees at saddle height, so one could ride along the trail and read God's word amidst His glorious surroundings. "As for me and my HORSE, we will serve the Lord!" This was a little play on words from the verse in Joshua 24:15(KJV) which says "As for me and my house, we will serve the Lord." "Some trust in horses, and some trust in chariots but we trust in the name of the Lord our God," Psalm 20:7. Revelation 19:14(KJV), "And the armies which were in heaven followed Him upon white horses, clothed in fine linen, white and clean." Psalm 119:105, "Your Word is a lamp for my feet and a light for my path."

Chapter Twenty-Two

No matter how full your life is, or how busy you are, everyone needs a close friend who knows everything about you, who you can confide in. I had left such dear ones in South Carolina, and I missed them so much. I was so busy now that I didn't have time to go to luncheons and out shopping, like I used to love to do with those precious women. I told the Lord that I needed a new friend who loved Him, and who loved horses too.

We hadn't been up and running very long when Linsey developed a painful toothache. We looked in the phonebook and called a random dentist. While he was in the chair, the dentist was being assisted by "Cindy" (to protect her privacy, this is not her real name). She was so sweet and personable. She had the gift of making everyone feel at ease immediately. Linsey began telling her about the recent events in our life and how we were now serving the Lord through horse ministry. He also told her about a great new start-up church we'd found in town.

Cindy was spellbound by his story and she shared that she'd not been attending church for a while, but needed to find another place to worship. She also loved horses. She'd owned a horse when she was a teenager, in California. The horse had lived at her beloved grandmother's farm and she had missed that chapter of her life for many years. Linsey invited her to visit our church and told her that she needed to meet up with me, that maybe we could ride together sometime. Soon, she did and we did. God brought me that precious friend. She'd had her own ups and downs in life. She was hurting from a very painful marriage. She loved the Lord with all of her heart and she was trusting God to heal her marriage, no matter how long it took.

When she met our mare, Sapphire, it was love at first sight for both of them. She would not ride any other horse. We spent many hours trail riding together and pouring our hearts out to each other. When we hosted programs at the farm, I would put her in charge of all of our volunteers while I was running around, making sure that all was going smoothly. We sat together in church every Sunday and she became a part of our weekly home Bible study. Linsey and I weren't able to get away very often, but whenever we could, Cindy would farm sit for all the horses, dogs, cats, chickens and the parrot. She was loved as much by the animals as she was by us.

Chapter Twenty-Three

S oon we were needing more horses. I placed an ad on the feed store bulletin board stating that we needed a sweet, well-trained, healthy horse for our ministry, who would be given regular love by many kids, great care, and lots of treats. God read that ad and inspired a local woman to help us acquire Sassy, a beautiful buckskin mare who was just what we were looking for. Originally, her name was "Sissy," but we changed it. We decided that she couldn't endure hours of having kids bounce around on her back like sacks of potatoes, and be a sissy.

Our mail carrier was a horsewoman too, and stopped by often to "talk horses" whenever she had a package to deliver. She eventually loaned us a big, sweet horse who was standing around in her pasture without a job, who she thought we could use. "PJ" was a real character. We decided "PJ" stood for practical joker, because his antics were hilarious.

As I mentioned earlier, we acquired twin Morgan geldings. Twins are rare in the horse world. They usually do not survive. However, We found the "Generals," as they became affectionately known. They were up in age, but perfect for the kids. They'd been used as Civil War re-enactors, thus their names, Generals Grant and Lee. Grant was the hardier of the two. Lee was a follower. I could always put my weaker student on Lee, because I knew that he would follow Grant wherever he went, and never be tempted to run off.

Rocky, King and Sapphire were working full time, and we took in two more horses that belonged to a lady who was going through a nasty divorce. She was worried that harm might come to them. We agreed to keep them for no charge, as long as we could use them for lessons. Over the years we lived at Full Circle Farm, twenty-eight horses graced our property at one time or another. Each one came with their own distinct "horsenality," and each was as precious and special as the kids who rode them.

Because older horses make the safest mounts for children, we shed many tears when we would lose them. Dear Blaze ended up with cancer. We sent him off for surgery, hoping it hadn't spread, but it had. He came back home for a few more months, and one cold night, after spending hours with him in his stall, he laid down, put his head in my lap and took his last breath. Some became unridable due to arthritis, and we'd keep them or find them a home where they could finish out their days with love and care. We had a wall in our basement recreation room we called the "Hall of Mane." On it were framed pictures of every horse that was a part of the ministry. These beloved four-legged "children" served the Lord as much as we did.

Once, a story about our ministry made the evening news. We were featured in the newspapers several times too. Pizza Hut came out one summer and donated pizzas for the "Fresh Air Kids" Program. The Fresh Air Kids are inner city kids from New York City. Some have never been out of the city. They are given the chance to visit rural areas for two weeks in the summer. This program exists throughout several of the mid-Atlantic states, and has been around for decades.

These children come to the area by bus, and are fostered out with local families. They have a ball. We hosted two little girls in our home the first year, but after that, we decided it would be a better idea to have the whole group out to the farm for a day of horseback riding, hayrides, food, fun and games. It was amazing to see the wonder in their eyes, as they experienced things they never had done before, such as run barefoot through soft, green grass, go on a hayride and ride a horse.

We hosted pre-schools, church groups and a Girl Scout troop. We arranged surprise birthday rides, and hosted many different ministry groups. I taught private lessons to a little girl who suffered from a degenerative muscular disease. She wore leg braces. She required frequent surgeries to help stretch her muscles. We were thrilled that her doctor said that the riding she was doing was helping her legs so much that she did not require as many surgeries. We allowed a young man to propose to his girlfriend on horseback. She said "yes"! At Christmastime, I led a little boy to Christ by taking him into one of the horse stalls and telling him how Jesus was born in a stable and then laid in a manger. Some came to Christ around the campfires we would have at the end of the day, while roasting hot dogs and sharing more stories about the love of Jesus. We were truly humbled to see what God was doing through our ministry.

Chapter Twenty-Four

It took a lot of volunteers to have these kinds of programs. My older students were such gems. I loved them beyond words and thought of them all as the daughters I never had. They knew and loved the horses and they knew what I expected. They spent countless hours helping and sweating in the hot sun, to share the love of God and the joy of horses with the wonderful people we served. We worked hard, but we had great fun and we created memories that will last a lifetime.

When I look back on each precious soul that was sent our way, though, there is one special family that stands out above the rest. When I first met "Sally" (not her real name), she sported the "Gothic" look, with black lipstick, piercings, chains and leather. Since so many of my students came from stricter homeschool families, Sally's look was a little different from what I was used to. She and her best friend, and her friend's brother signed up together. The girls were fourteen at the time. Despite their looks, they were as sweet as could be, and they were horse crazy. I loved them immediately. They rarely missed a lesson, and I was also beginning to get to know their parents. The brother and sister came from a family who regularly attended church and their godly grandmother lived with them.

Sally's mother, "Tory"(not her real name), had other grown children from other marriages. I felt such a connection to them from the start, but it was clear that they did not know the Lord, and that they had endured many heartbreaks in their lives. Tory would usually stay in her SUV, parked close to the arena so she could watch Sally ride. Most of the time she kept to herself, unless I specifically approached her. I enjoyed our conversations when we had the chance, and I remember her telling me once that I made her want to be a better person. That meant so much to me. I hope it was the Lord Jesus shining through me that she saw. The kids progressed quickly and became valued volunteers for our group ministry programs. They soaked up the weekly devotional stories that I shared, and they were always so kind and respectful.

Our niece Laurel, and her husband became owners of a Chick Fil-A restaurant, and scheduled an employee retreat at our farm one weekend. There was riding, hayrides, a cookout and a campfire. Laurel shared her life story around the fire that evening, about how she had accepted Christ while living with us in South Carolina, and what Jesus meant to her. When she was finished, Linsey had the group bow their heads. He prayed, and gave the attendees a chance to make a commitment to the Lord. Sally was one of two, who responded. We were elated! It was obvious from that day on, that Sally loved the Lord and wanted to serve God. Soon, Tory, and Sally's sister began attending church with us and also became a part of our weekly home Bible study. Tory accepted Christ one Sunday at church, and soon Sally's sister followed. Next, her sister led her friend to Christ. It was so amazing. We were seeing dramatic changes and newfound joy in their lives. All three of them were baptized at the YMCA pool that our church used for such purposes. Linsey and I were honored to be able to be in the water with them that day. What a thrill! They had become precious members of our family.

Tory grew up in New England and she and her family went back for a vacation. While there, they met Tory's old friend, a man who, at one time, had been the love of her life. They all had a great time. It was eerily obvious to Paul (not his real name) how much Sally looked like him. When he saw a baby picture of her and noticed the date of her birth, he came to the earth-shattering realization that Sally had to be his daughter. When he confronted Tory, she admitted the truth. She had never told him or Sally. Her current husband thought Sally was his own daughter.

When Sally learned the truth, she was elated to know who she really was, and a close bond developed between her and her real father. He had been married and had sons, but never a daughter. He wanted to get to know her and spend time with her. When he learned how much she loved horses, he bought her a lovely gelding, "Merlin," who was badly in need of a home. Sadly, after he was shipped to our farm, he only lived one month. He was very sick and Paul and Sally had been cruelly taken advantage of. Sally was devastated and needed to find another horse. There was a rescue farm nearby where horses were brought in and rehabilitated and ultimately placed in "forever" homes. It's a top-rate operation, and they were responsible for matching Sally to "Snickers." Snickers came to live at Full Circle Farm and a strong bond developed between Sally and her beautiful Thoroughbred. Paul showered his daughter with a new saddle, bridle, brushes and everything he could think of that she would have need of.

Paul made frequent trips to Virginia and came out to the farm often, but he still lived in New England. On Thanksgiving day of that year, while back home, he lost control of his car, hit a tree, and died. Life had been growing more and more bumpy for Tory and her husband since Paul had come into their lives and the truth about Sally was learned. The entire family began to spin out of control. Tory found counseling for Sally to help her with the intense anguish that she was suffering. A doctor got involved and drugs were prescribed. No one drug seemed to dull Sally's pain. On each trip back to the doctor, additional drugs were prescribed. Sally came out to the farm less and less, and they had all quit coming to church and to Bible study. When I did see her, she looked like a zombie.

She knew the drugs were affecting her severely and she shared with me more than once, her desire to get off of them. Her doctor did not agree.

I'll never forget the day she and her boyfriend came out, and she questioned me about the syringes and needles that I kept in my equine medicine chest. She said that one of her dogs was sick and had need of them. My heart was breaking. I put a lock on the medicine chest immediately, and told her that if her dog needed injections, her vet would provide them. I loved her so much and I tried to talk to her. I prayed and prayed.

One weekend, Sally and her boyfriend had gone to several parties. Sally, high on prescription drugs, assaulted two different individuals. There was an arrest, later a trial, and she was sentenced to jail. As horrific as it was, it was God's way to rescue them all. He cleansed her physically and spiritually. She was taken off the pills cold turkey and she suffered no ill effects, which was miraculous in itself. The first time we went to visit her was very traumatic. Sally was so ashamed, and when we saw her through the glass in her orange jumpsuit, it was hard to speak. We were all stricken with unbearable pain and sadness. Our pastor stepped in and began visiting her each week, in addition to her family. I began writing her letters instead, and sending her devotional books. I'd even found some that were horse themed.

Soon Sally began sharing Christ in jail. She became the leader of a Bible study and a prayer time there. God had gotten her attention and she was hungry for scripture. She was sorry, and determined to come through her experience a changed young woman, fully devoted to the Lord like never before. I would like to share a few excerpts from some of her letters:

"I'm sorry you had to sit in court and listen to what a horrible person I used to be. I know it was really hard on y'all. I'm ok though. I know there's still things God needs me to do and people I can help. I miss you so very much. I'm so thankful for our pastor and the whole church. People who don't even know me take the time to pray and write. I can't even get "friends" of mine that I've known for years to write. I'm so glad God put you in my life. I thank Him always for you and Linsey. I gave my testimony here last Sunday. Over half the girls in here sat and listened, even some who I've never heard talk about God started crying. I am so very blessed. God is so good! This girl in here got her Dad to print out lyrics to a song called "Thank you," by Ray Boltz. I'm going to write down the last part because it is totally how I feel about y'all. It says "thank you, for giving to the Lord. I am so glad you gave." I honestly don't think you will ever know the impact you have made on not only my life, but also on everyone who has ever had the privilege of meeting you. Thank you for never giving up on me. I love you more than any words in the English language could ever explain! I miss you but God's timing is perfect!"

"These aren't just words on paper. I'm not going to let ya'll down. I know a lot of people missed the "Sally before meds", but as much as everyone missed the old me, I missed her more. I hated who I had turned into, I didn't know how to go back. I still have kinks to work out, but I just wanted to assure you that hollow, zombie Sally is gone. It's me again and I can't wait to prove it."

"I am still leading devotions. The other day a woman who just got sentenced to a year in prison came up to me and told me how good I was doing and that as much as she's praying I get to go home soon, devotions won't be the same once I'm gone. Another girl who doesn't even attend devotions said that she's never gone to church before and said it would feel wrong to start now. I told her we all have to start somewhere, and what better way to insure that you won't have to come back here, than to give your life to Jesus and let Him take control of your life! I don't know how some of these girls do it. Some have been in and out of prison for years. I'm blessed that this is my first and last time. My heart breaks for those people."

"Free on the inside...today I am blessed to say that God has chased my demons away! If you look in my eyes you will see nothing but love and purity. If I shall stumble or if I should fall, Jesus Christ will be the name that I call. And when God seems the furthest away, look to the sky and pray, pray pray! He won't leave you out in the dark or the cold. He'll lift you up and restore your soul. When you forsake Him...when, not if, you can ask for forgiveness, what a beautiful gift. Life on this earth goes by way too fast. I've been yearning for You, Lord, I'm free at last!"

As she said, after serving ten months, she was freed, not only by the state of Virginia, but by the Lord Jesus Himself. She became an active member of her church. She began coming back to the farm to see Snickers. That horse had deeply mourned her absence, and practically danced, the day they were reunited. She told her old friends she needed to begin a new lifestyle and it did not include them. She found a new job and a place to live. She eventually left her boyfriend, who was also a bad influence on her.

As is said so often, serving and loving others brings US more joy than it brings the ones we pour ourselves into. I wouldn't be the person I am today had it not been for Sally and her family. God used them so very much in my life. I am positive that one of the main reasons God sent us to Virginia, was to share Christ with them. There is a Bible story that shows how God often sends His children on such sacred missions. This story is in Acts 8:26-40. A man was traveling across the desert, reading God's word along the way, and he was having trouble understanding it. Philip, an evangelist, was told by an angel to go to the road from Jerusalem to Gaza, and there he would meet this Ethiopian eunuch. The man was sitting in his chariot, reading in the book of Isaiah, and had stopped.

The angel told Philip to go to the chariot and stay near it. Philip then asked the man if he understood what he was reading. "How can I," he said, "unless someone explains it." So Philip came and sat with him. He was reading Isaiah 53:7-8, which says "He was oppressed and afflicted, yet he did not open his mouth; he was led like a lamb to the slaughter." The man asked Philip who was being spoken of. Philip told him it was speaking of Jesus and he shared the good news of the gospel with him. They traveled along and came to some water, and the man asked Philip why he shouldn't be baptized. Both men went into the water and Philip baptized him. What a divine detour that turned out to be. Our Lord will indeed leave the ninety-nine sheep to go and rescue even one that strays or needs Him.

As of this writing, Sally is married to a wonderful young man. They own a small farm where Snickers still lives, along with a second horse. She's following in my footsteps, with a desire to work with kids and teach riding. She and her husband just celebrated the first birthday of their darling daughter. Linsey and I are unofficial grandparents! Linsey is "Grampy" and I'm "GramV." When we heard the wonderful news that Sally was expecting, I wrote her the following poem. We will be eternally grateful that she escaped the deadly detour she was on, and headed for God's best destination for her life and the lives of her family. I truly believe that one day, Sally will be sharing her testimony again, and God will be using her to rescue more lives and point them to our wonderful Savior.

Chapter Twenty-four

FOR SALLY

Vicki Borders
2018

It was not a bloodline or a family tree that bound me to you and you to me
Family ties are precious, though, I so agree!
They say "blood is thicker than water" but our bond? It was of the heavenly Father
He knew it all, from eons past that our special bond was going to last
Through galloping days with the wind in our hair to pain so intense we could hardly bear.
But our hearts were strong and our love was true
The prayers for each other helped see us through.
And now it seems we've passed great tests and God is pouring out His best
Friends and family, tranquil farms, the love overflows from our Father's arms
A precious new life is coming your way to complete your joy and bless your days
The Father knew we'd not want to miss out
It's a "full circle" thing, without a doubt, to be back home so we could share
In the joys and blessings year after year
No matter how "we" came to be...We praise Him because we are family!

Chapter Twenty-Five

In October 2010, Joshua married the love of his life. He met his beautiful bride at a job he only held a short time, in Lynchburg, Virginia. It's evident that God placed him there specifically to meet his beautiful Emily. She grew up on Long Island, New York, in a large, loving Christian family.

When they married, we hosted their rehearsal dinner at our farm. It was so much fun! We set up long tables, supported on the ends by hay bales, with colorful tablecloths, candles and lights strung overhead. We had a bonfire, Southern barbecue, and a karaoke machine set up beneath our deck. We heard later that the New York relatives weren't too sure about this "hoe-down" of an event, but after it was over, they talked about the good time they had for months.

Josh and Emily set up their new life in downtown Lynchburg, in an historic apartment building that at one time had been a department store. They soon added a Bassett Hound puppy, "Ulysses S. Grant," to their home. Our first "grand dog."

Eventually they moved back to Charleston, South Carolina. Josh missed his longtime friends, and the lure of the Holy City. Emily, being a Civil War buff, loves being in a place where so much of that history unfolded. Josh first went back to work with a local television news team. One of his first assignments was covering the horrific church shooting in Charleston, in June of

2015. Not only was it dangerous work, but the pain and reality of the day-to-day filming of life in our world, with its many tragedies, was not what Josh wanted to do with the rest of his life. God provided a great new job for him where he still uses his video and writing talents in a company that serves others and provides him much peace and fulfillment.

Chapter Twenty-Six

J eremy eventually moved from Texas to New York City. He had written, sung and acted in a musical while in Texas, and he found he liked acting so much that he wanted to go to the "Big Apple" and see if God might be leading him in that direction. He got some bit parts on television shows such as "Ugly Betty" and "Law & Order" and he appeared as an extra in several movies. He won a piano competition and was honored to play at Carnegie Hall twice. These "honors" did not pay the bills, however. Soon Jeremy ended up on our doorstep, a true "starving artist." He insisted that this move had not been a detour. He was certain that God had used the New York experience to direct his life in some very important ways, and it's clear that He did.

With Jeremy back in Virginia, progress was slow at first, but God eventually opened up a door for him to become a praise and worship leader at two different churches. The positions were only part-time. He found that he loved leading congregations and choirs, and ushering them into worshipping the Lord. He wrote praise songs and made some excellent music videos. Because the churches were small though, he was unable to earn enough to live on. He didn't want to live with us forever, so he explored every possibility for employment.

God next opened an opportunity for him to work as an entertainer with Carnival Cruise Lines. He began going out to sea for usually three months at a time. He worked about three to five hours, six out of seven days a week, in the piano bar and in the Broadway-type productions that were performed onboard. On nights when he played in the piano bar, in exchange for tips, he gave the guests a cd of his music. At the end of this cd was a verbal plan of salvation. He had laminated copies of all the songs in his repertoire available so passengers could peruse through it and make requests. On that list, among songs of every genre, were praise and worship songs. I'm sure it wasn't common to hear songs lifting up the Lord on many of the other Carnival ships. He loved the opportunity to travel to so many exotic places and meet such interesting people.

For a young, single Christian man though, being continuously out to sea was not the life that Jeremy desired to live forever. He was realizing he had a true passion to lead praise and worship full time. After a couple years, he came back to Virginia again, determined to see if God would open a door. Because of the experience God had allowed him to have on the cruise ships, much larger churches were now interested in him.

There was a position for a praise and worship leader at a sizable church in Atlanta, Georgia. Having lived in the south for so long, he had hoped for it to be a fit, but it wasn't.

Several other opportunities presented themselves, including one in Northern Michigan. This location, just one hour south of Canada, was the total opposite of a destination like Atlanta. They receive an average of 141" of snow each year. It is a vacation spot, peppered with resorts and ski slopes. In the summer the many lakes attract vacationers who love fishing, boating and water sports and the area abounds with wooded trails for cycling, hiking, four-wheeling and horseback riding.

The church Jeremy was going to interview at was one of the largest in the area, running over one thousand members, with two services each Sunday, and it was both televised and on the radio. The position was for a Director of Music. Jeremy was interviewed by the pastor, the search committee and the board of elders. He filled out an in-depth application which asked intimate questions and delved deeply into his personal life. He was hired for the position.

He moved to Michigan, and dove into his work. He needed a place to live, so two different families from the church graciously opened their homes to him until he could find something suitable. On his first Sunday in charge, he met a talented couple who told him they felt led to move there from farther north in order to be on the team. He had two drummers, a base, a lead and an acoustic guitarist, a keyboard player, a trumpeter and a violinist, not to mention many very talented singers, all who were excited and eager to join the team and serve the Lord. Jeremy was in his element, and he was thrilled to see that the worship music being offered to our Lord was fulfilling his high expectations. Church members began sharing their gratitude for a deeper, more meaningful worship experience than they had experienced at the church before.

He started working on his first big project immediately, which was the "Christmas Spectacular," to be presented on two evenings in mid-December. This was a huge undertaking, but Jeremy was motivated and excited to include all the talent available to him throughout the entire church, from youngsters to older adults, to bring a truly remarkable Christmas celebration to the community. Jeremy thrived on this type of challenge and many hours of practice and planning by all were devoted to this program.

Chapter Twenty-Seven

Time flies when you're having fun, right? When we first bought our farm, we asked the Lord for ten good years there. We knew we'd taken on a huge financial burden with our property, and that once Linsey retired, we would never be able to keep up with the mortgage payments. We felt that the farm belonged to the Lord anyways, and we would be His instruments there as long as it pleased Him. By the time we were approaching twelve years, we could see the writing on the wall. It was time to begin thinking of retirement.

Linsey was growing tired from the many business miles he was driving every month. It was taking a toll on his body. We had both suffered tick-related illnesses also. When he was away, it was up to me, alone, to shovel manure, clean stalls, feed and keep up with all the other work that multiple horses require, in addition to my lesson program. We also had chickens and a good-sized veggie garden that provided us food for most of every winter, and it all required a lot of work. We had always managed completely on our own with no hired help.

My mother had recently come to live with us, for what was to be the last five years of her life. She was in her late eighties when she arrived, and she had begun falling too often, first breaking a wrist, then an ankle. She'd already had a hip replaced and she was wracked with painful arthritis and the beginnings of congestive heart failure. My sister and I thought that she needed to sell her condo in Ohio and come to Virginia to live with us before she suffered any more physical damage. She had been close to my sister for many years and I really wanted to have her with us. I still hoped to forge a closer relationship with her.

We were thankful that she agreed to come. There were definitely some precious moments, but there were many trying days. She was in so much pain that it broke my heart.

I felt so helpless. I think at times she enjoyed being with us, but she missed Ohio so much that she never really considered being with us as home. She usually sat with our group when we had our weekly Bible study and I loved how our friends doted over her. She loved our cat, Callie, who would spend many an hour on her lap, keeping her warm and purring up a storm. She enjoyed spending time with Josh, Emily and Jeremy whenever they were home. I tried so hard to determine whether or not she truly had a relationship with Jesus Christ. She said she did, but it was not easily visible. This was never a topic that she felt comfortable discussing.

Eventually, we placed our farm on the market. What a bittersweet decision. Full Circle Farm held such memories, miracles, and joy. I looked forward to the next chapter in our life though. I was anticipating the day when Linsey would no longer have to travel and we could be retired, yet still be young and healthy enough to enjoy our horses, travel, and do whatever retired folks do. Once the "for sale" sign went into the yard, the months passed and we had lookers, but no offers. We realized that horse farms would not attract a large slice of buyers, but we stayed hopeful. We began to downsize our herd. Those who boarded with us needed to find new homes for their animals, and thankfully, we found amazing homes for our own horses through selling and/or donating them to very special owners.

As a token of my love and affection for my friend Cindy, I gave Sapphire to her. I couldn't imagine the two of them ever being separated.

We planned to have just one more horse each, for retirement. We were not ready to be completely horseless. I found "Buck," a Tennessee Walking Horse who channeled "Mr. Ed." Buck is one of the most amazing horses I have ever known, and God showed up and showed off when He allowed him to be my last horse. Linsey found "Apache," an older Appaloosa, as bomb-proof as they come. Apache and Buck became good buddies, and together the four of us enjoyed the trails. We knew that wherever we ended up, we would happily ride off into retirement.

Mom's health continued to deteriorate and soon Hospice was called in. She was not bedridden yet. She wanted to go to Ohio to visit my sister, which turned out to be the last three months of her life. The night before we left to drive her there, she fell in the bathroom and cracked a rib. It was a very painful trip for her. My dear sister had Hospice in place as soon as she arrived, and not long after she got settled in, she did become bedridden.

During her last weeks she grew more and more agitated. The Hospice worker suggested that perhaps there were unaddressed issues in her life that she wanted to confront. Was it possible that she wanted to see me once more, they wondered? Unfortunately, we were not able to make the trip. However, my sister suggested that maybe we could "Skype." My brother-in-law set it up, and Mom and I talked, via our computers. She never really looked at the screen, she was so very weak. I told her how much I loved her, and I thanked her for taking care of my sister and I all the years since we'd lost our dad, and how hard we knew she'd worked to provide for us. I told her that it was ok to quit fighting. She was ninety-four years old, and in unbearable pain. I told her that she wouldn't have to worry about my sister and me, that we would stay close and look out for one another. I told her to reach out to Jesus and take His hand when He came for her, that it was ok to go with Him and that she would finally have peace, joy and absence of pain. My sister said that Mom heard my words and smiled. In less than forty-eight hours, she was gone. I hope and pray that the Lord Jesus personally came and offered His hand to her and that she eagerly grasped it and arrived safely in heaven. I'll never know for sure until I arrive there myself, but I felt that the Lord gave me that unforgettable time with her as an indication that she truly did know Him.

Chapter Twenty-Eight

After Mom passed, we decided to take a trip to Michigan to visit Jeremy to check out his new life. It was autumn, and the leaves were spectacular.

The stark white of the many Birch trees was so beautiful, amidst the vivid colors. We'd never lived anywhere where Birch trees existed. I've never seen much of Canada, but to me, the landscape made me feel as if we were there. We saw groups on their four-wheelers, trekking along the many trails that parallel the roads before they cut back into the woods. We saw an elk herd and many nice resorts, and we were blown away by the abundance of lakes. There was everything outdoor-loving people could ask for.

On Sunday, we visited the church. We were so proud of Jeremy and his leadership. We had been watching the services over the internet ever since he left, but it was so amazing to be there in person. We met the pastor and told him how much we enjoyed his Bible teaching. The people were friendly and we felt so welcome.

During our visit, Jeremy expressed to us that he would love it if we would move to Michigan when the farm sold. Boy, were we taken aback. He said he'd like us to be near, and also join the praise team. It'd been years since I'd had any opportunity to sing and play, and I'd been missing that for a long time.

Evidently, he'd been seriously praying about this for some time. It seemed like a wonderful church with a great mix of age groups and lots of activities to be a part of. We all talked and prayed a lot about it, wondering if that was why our farm had not sold in over ten months. Our plan had been to find a much smaller home and farm and stay in Virginia, close to our friends and our church there. By the time we got back home, we decided to change our direction and see what God would do. Three weeks later, after a surge in showings, the farm sold. We felt this was our answer. Wouldn't embracing ONE MORE adventurous destination be a great way to embark on retirement?

Chapter Twenty-Nine

It would be winter soon. That's not such an issue in Central Virginia, but we knew that it could be a huge issue in Northern Michigan. We purchased a home, and our life immediately became a whirlwind, trying to pack and move and arrive there before December 15th, which was the first night of Jeremy's"Christmas Spectacular." We didn't want to miss it. We shipped Buck and Apache a couple of weeks before we left so they could be safe and settled into the boarding stable that would be their new home.

We were given a heart wrenching going away party by about twenty-five or so of our dearest friends, complete with tears, gifts and promises on all of our parts to keep in touch, knowing that we would all miss each other so much. I'm sure that most of our friends thought we were crazy. They reminded us that most retirees head to Florida! We honestly did have mixed feelings about this abrupt decision, but we knew God was leading us.

On the day we left Virginia, our SUV was packed to the ceiling, along with our two huge dogs and the parrot in his travel cage. It was snowing on the way North. As we made it farther and farther, it got worse. When we arrived in our new town, it was a total "whiteout." It surely had been many, many years since we'd seen this kind of a scene through a windshield.

We thought we had found our exit off the interstate, but we couldn't be positive, due to the swirling wind and snow. We said a quick prayer and veered off, hoping for the best. God was guiding us.

We stayed at a hotel for the first two nights. The weather was so bad. We weren't positive that the hotel we stopped at was pet-friendly, and we were too exhausted to search far and wide for one in an area unknown to us. Smuggling the dogs in wasn't such an issue, but we were fervently praying that the guests in the rooms closest to ours wouldn't hear our crazy parrot loudly yelling things like "Peekaboo"! "Whatcha doing?" "Praise the Looooooooord!" "Crunch wants out!" The movers were to arrive the next day with our furniture, but they got stuck, due to the storm, and were delayed another day. When they did arrive, the snow was too deep on our cul de sac, so our furniture had to be ferried from the large moving van parked down on the main road, to a smaller truck that could navigate up to our home. We were sure that all of our stuff would be broken to bits. There was over three feet of snow on the ground and even more on our back deck.

This was a real culture shock for us "Southern marshmallows." Needless to say, our first major purchase was a heavy-duty snow-blower and winter wardrobes fit for Nanook of the North.

We were road-weary and not able to be as spruced-up as we'd have liked, but we made it to the Christmas Spectacular. Spectacular it was. There was nothing about the music, singing, dancing, or sets that didn't rival any true Broadway performance. We were busting our buttons! We were so proud of the whole group. It was said that the church had never experienced a program of that calibre.

The winter passed quickly because we were busy unpacking, exploring our new locale and settling in. We bought snow-shoes and went hiking, and we were planning to learn to cross-country ski. We were seriously considering buying a couple of snowmobiles. There were so many folks using them on the neighborhood trails that surrounded us, that it often sounded like a swarm of bees.

Jeremy now lived with us. He'd been trying to buy a house, but he was falling short of qualifying for a loan, especially since he was new to the area and to his job. Our home had an efficiency apartment in the basement with its own entrance, so it worked out perfectly. It truly was a joyful time for the three of us. Jeremy had made good friends, and he often invited them over to join in for fun and board games. The stable had an indoor riding arena, so we could enjoy the horses even when the snow was up to our back pockets. The horses were doing well and the stable was not far away.

It wasn't long until we joined the praise team. It was fun to be singing again and feeling a part of the ministry. Soon Jeremy asked me to play my guitar and sing a solo at the close of a service. Oh my! I was honored that he thought I could con-tribute and be a blessing but I was terrified. I was feeling quite comfortable being in the group of background singers. This church was large and it was televised. I tried to get out of it, but Jeremy would not back down. I practiced the song so much I could sing it in my sleep, and when that Sunday came, I was almost physically ill. I was "rusty" and it'd been a long time since my Christian Women's Club speaking and singing days. I wasn't sure if I was supposed to be retired from this phase too. God was so amazing. When I opened my mouth, peace flooded my soul and I truly thought only of my love for Jesus, serving Him, and the beautiful words to the song. The people loved it. I was so humbled and touched. This opened new doors for me to occasionally sing my own songs in several different settings within the church. It was such a gift from the Lord for me to be able to share my heart in this way. It was definitely another full circle.

Chapter Thirty

S oon spring came and we decided to buy a fishing boat. Linsey had been wanting one for a long time. I prayed and asked the Lord if He would help me to support this new venture, because for so many years, Linsey supported my horse addiction, which took up most of our free time and money. It was time for me to step up and pour myself into something that he really wanted to do. We found the perfect, gently-used boat, and we began heading out to the many lakes that were just minutes away from our home. We both loved it.

I'll never forget one of our first trips. We were catching some large Bass. We were laughing and shrieking, taking pictures and holding them up, so proud of our efforts. We noticed this woman intently watching us from the dock where we'd put the boat in, afar off. We saw her watching us from another spot also, where we'd caught a couple of big fish as well. When it was time to call it a day, we were trying to head the boat back, using just our trolling motor. We had not been able to start the larger motor. It was going to need to be serviced. The troller usually worked fine, but on this day, a strong wind came up and the little motor was not enabling us to make much headway. We'd move forward a little, and then the boat would be blown back around in a circle. We were frustrated because it was taking forever. After about forty-five minutes of trying, we noticed that the lady watching us seemed to give up and leave. Strange! Later, we realized what had happened. There are strict fishing laws in Michigan. We had read the guide when we got our licenses, but somehow we missed the fact that we were a week EARLY for Bass season. The mysterious lady was probably a DNR (Department of Natural Resources) Agent who could have heavily fined us for our mistake.

God stirred up a mighty wind to protect us that day. We were much more careful after that. I fried our catch up with garlic, cornmeal and olive oil. Those "illegal" fish sure tasted good.

Chapter Thirty-One

W e'd only been in town a couple of months when I joined
a women's winter Bible study at the church, taught
by our pastor's wife. I was a little shy because I hardly knew
anyone, but I met the nicest ladies. One of them, who God
clearly intended for me to meet, was "Marilyn"(not her real
name). Although she was not born in Michigan, she had lived
in the state much of her life. She had a Master's degree in psychology and had worked for years in the counseling field. She
had recently retired and was planning to move to a beautiful
senior housing facility, but there was a waiting list. She'd been
house-sitting for a friend who spent the winters in Florida, and
it wouldn't be long until her friend would be back and she'd
need a place to live.

When her house-sitting period ended, she opted to camp.
She owned a nice, two-bedroom tent. She loved the outdoors
and she knew the folks who managed the county campground,
which was situated on a gorgeous lake. She lived very simply,
and all of her possessions could fit into her SUV, including
Snowy, her sweetheart of a cat. We were so fascinated by
Marilyn and her bravery. I could have never camped by myself
in a tent, not knowing how long it would be until I found permanent housing. She lived every moment trusting the Lord.
We helped her move and set up her tent. She had to change

campsites occasionally, so whenever she did, we would go out and help her gather up all of her belongings, take down the tent, and put it back up at the next site. She camped the entire summer.

Marilyn became like a sister to us. Her love for the Lord radiated from her, and she spent hours a day in prayer. She also joined the praise team at church. She was so much fun to be with. We began walking together once a week, and often she'd come over and spend almost the whole day with us, playing cards, playing with the dogs and having a great time. We spent holidays together and she house-sat for us when we took trips.

We were so excited to help her move into her beautiful new apartment, when the day finally came. When we moved to Michigan we brought extra furniture, thinking that Jeremy could use it when he was able to purchase a house. Since he was not having good luck with that, and he honestly was not interested in our stuff, we decided to bless Marilyn with it. We were able to nearly completely furnish her one bedroom place. It was really neat and she was so happy. What could have been a starkly appointed abode, was instantly homey and cozy. God is so good! He knew that we brought those things to Michigan for Marilyn, and not for Jeremy. What a miracle it was that God brought "Auntie Marilyn" into our life.

Chapter Thirty-Two

A nd then there was "Big Ticket." Big Ticket is nearly a week-long annual Christian music festival. It attracts thousands of people, youth groups and churches from all over the country. People pour into town. Nationally known Christian artists are featured, as well as speakers, food, and merchandise tents. There are fun things to do for kids of all ages and the whole affair is an opportunity to charge your Christian battery.

The man who organized this event attended the church. Jeremy loved his whole family. He gave their daughter piano lessons. It wasn't long until he was told that he was going to be given the opportunity to play on the Main Stage, on opening day, and be featured as a new artist. What a thrill that was for him.

He got to play on the same stage that Mac Powell, from Third Day, Chris Tomlin, For King & Country, Skillet, Michael W. Smith, and many more played on that week.

He had his own merchandise table and sold some of his cds and he met so many wonderful people. He was even interviewed on the radio. For him, it ranked right up there with playing at Carnegie Hall. We got backstage passes and had a blast. We felt like groupies. We were so proud of him and the others from church who were a part of his band.

Chapter Thirty-Three

J eremy loved being a part of the ministry of this church. He worked long hours and gave 110%. He was asked if he would work with the teens, leading worship occasionally in their youth room. This room was large, complete with a small stage. A couple in the church built beautiful backdrops for use on the main auditorium stage. Once a new backdrop was created, the older ones were stored away, so Jeremy set to work using pieces from one of the older sets to really "pop" this stage for them. He enlisted the help of a couple of the youth and they were quite pleased with the results.

The room hadn't been painted or re-carpeted in years, and Jeremy thought it could really use a facelift. He wanted to surprise the kids with his "gift" of updating the entire space. His heart was in the right place, but he did not have permission to do anything more than the work on the stage. What became catastrophic was that he incorporated the use of spray paint in his design project. The fumes from the paint seeped into the walls and carpet. It was learned later that, because the weather was still cool and the furnace was still running, had there been a spark of any kind, it's possible that the building could have gone up in flames.

The building committee and the adult youth leaders were understandably incensed at what Jeremy had done. He was verbally reprimanded. It was estimated by the insurance company that thousands of dollars of damage was done. However, our God was so gracious and merciful. The insurance company covered a huge portion of the damage. The youth room was ultimately re-carpeted, which was needed all along, and it was restored to a wonderful new level. A letter was sent to the entire church body, explaining what Jeremy had done. Jeremy, too, included a personal, written apology. In the letter, the pastor wrote that Jeremy's intentions had been good and his heart was in the right place. He went on to say that God had ultimately blessed the church and the youth room with the way it all had turned out. It was another example of Romans 8:28, "And we know that in all things God works for the good of those who love him, who have been called according to his purpose." Eventually it all blew over, and Jeremy was jokingly called "Rembrandt" by a few, and warned never to touch spray paints again.

Chapter Thirty-Four

We were really wanting to make a trip to South Carolina to see Josh and Emily. They had moved back to Charleston, and had been down there nearly two years. When they moved, my mom was living with us, and as her health grew worse we couldn't leave her. Then, after she passed, we were in the process of moving to Michigan.

Just when we finally found a good date for our trip, Josh called with horrifying news. He'd been diagnosed with colon cancer at the age of thirty-five. He'd been having mild stomach issues for years, but more serious symptoms were presenting themselves. He underwent tests, a biopsy, and then surgery was scheduled. He was naturally terrified and uncertain of his future. He wasn't sure of our family's medical history, and his doctor wanted the information to include in his records. It was sad to dig it all out and bring back those memories. He was only a fourth-grader when I was diagnosed with breast cancer. It was even sadder that now Josh was facing cancer at as young an age as I had been when I faced it. We wanted to be there by his side when he had the surgery, but Josh really wanted us to wait and come when he was recovered, so we could have fun together in Charleston. It was hard, but we waited.

Our God is an awesome God. John 11:4 says "This sickness will not end in death. No, it is for God's glory so that God's Son may be glorified through it."

That was the case for Josh, just as it had been for me. How we praised and thanked Him that He chose to heal Josh in such an amazing way. The cancer was caught so early that there was no need of radiation or chemotherapy. Miraculous! He was on complete rest for the first week, post-op, then he was allowed to work from home for a while after that.

It wasn't long until he was fully functional and feeling well again. We made our visit the first of November. The weather was wonderful in Charleston. Now that we lived in Northern Michigan, it was a new sensation to sweat and feel humidity again. As Josh had hoped, we spent lots of time wandering the historic streets, going to the Farmers' Market, eating at unique restaurants, playing games and spoiling our "grand dog." who we had missed as much as the kids. On Sunday, we all attended church together, where Josh plays and sings on the worship team. We had missed them so much and it was a great visit in every way.

Chapter Thirty-Five

Is there ever church drama? Do bears sleep in the woods? Is the sky blue? When leading talented musicians, invariably everyone has their own ideas about how music should be chosen, played and presented. The church in Michigan was no different. There were discussions, and at times there were clashes. Everyone cannot be pleased and in the end, the God-appointed leader has to do what is best for the team, according to his vision. The apostle Paul said to young Timothy in 1Timothy 4:12 "Don't let anyone look down on you because you are young, but set an example for the believers in speech, in conduct, in love, in faith and in purity." In Jeremy's case, this did happen. There were older members of the team who did not always like his ideas. They were resistant to change.

There was the issue of his "eligible bachelor" status as well. The girls were quite attentive. Feelings got hurt when Jeremy would express to them that his intentions were strictly friendship. This happened more than once. There was one young woman in particular, who Jeremy highly regarded as a close friend. They spent hours together. He bought a four-wheeler. He is a thrill seeker, and she loved flying along the trails with him. We liked her, and hoped that maybe something more might develop, but he did not feel that she was "the one." Once she understood this, the friendship was over and some hurtful lies were spread. We learned later that this was not the first time she had been so vindictive.

There was another situation that involved a power struggle between Jeremy and one of the featured singers, who never felt she had enough exposure, even though she was "front and center" almost every Sunday morning. Several of her children were talented musicians who served on the team as well. Her children were highly regarded and contributed greatly. Sometime after Christmas, one of them was involved in a serious snowmobiling accident. It was thought at first that he might be paralyzed as a result of his injuries. The church prayed and pled to the Lord for his healing. His mother stayed by his side at the hospital for weeks, and meals were made and taken to the rest of the family on a regular basis. Jeremy was so moved by God's hand and the miraculous healing that took place, that he wrote a new song in this boy's honor. It was a song that was sung by the praise team often.

I RECEIVE YOUR MIRACLES

by Jeremy Ray Borders

I receive Your miracles, I receive Your healing power.
I receive Your faithfulness in my life.
I receive Your promises, I put on Your joy
I will live by Your sacrifice in my life.

Come down, come now, come down, come down from
heaven now
Come down, come now, come down, come down from
heaven now.

I receive Your miracles, I receive Your healing power
I am saved by Your faithfulness, because You died.
I receive Your promises, I put on Your joy
And every season I sing and shout, You saved my life!

Come down, come now, come down, come down from
heaven now
Come down, come now, come down, come down from
heaven now

Come down, come now, come down, come down from
heaven now
Come down, come now, come down, come down from
heaven now

Jeremy had so many heart to heart talks with this woman.
She wanted more control of the team and constantly pushed
her ideas. She often was rude and defiant and confronted him

between church services, which was so disrespectful. Her jealousy, resentment and lack of self-control escalated. She set the wheels in motion which ultimately cost Jeremy his position. It was for her son that we pled to the Lord, for mercy and healing, and it was my son who she tried to destroy. There were so many more details to this turn of events, that another book could be written. There are two sides to every story, but both sides are comprised of the words of people. We looked to God and His word. It was our only comfort. We could not understand why this happened, but we knew that God was still in control and that He would lead our family.

Jeremy packed up and left Michigan with our blessing, but we were left feeling completely alone, in a place that once held such happiness and promise. We'd been really happy. We truly thought this would be our final earthly destination. Our many friends back in Virginia were appalled to hear about what had happened, and they urged us to come back home. We were told over and over that we were loved and missed. We prayed, and it was easy to hear the answer. We placed our home on the market immediately. This would mean yet another move, in just fifteen months' time. Were we sorry that we came to Michigan? Did we think we made a mistake in hearing the Lord? No! Even though it ended in heartbreak, we never doubted that God intended for us to be there for our son. Our relationship with Jeremy grew stronger than ever during our months there. We had some wonderful times, met some great people, enjoyed exploring a part of the country we may have never seen, and we gave our time and talents to the Lord, in serving Him.

If we needed any more confirmation as to what we should do next, one morning during his prayer and study time, Linsey received it. He was thinking about a specific Bible story that mirrored just how he was feeling. He knew the story, but not the "address." He really wanted to read it. He opened his Bible, and there it was, on the first try. He felt such a touch from the Master.

The passage he was looking for was in Luke, Chapter10, which says: "After this the Lord appointed seventy-two others and sent them two by two ahead of Him to every town and place where He was about to go. He told them 'the harvest is plentiful but the workers are few. Ask the Lord of the harvest, therefore to send out workers into His harvest field. Go! I am sending you out like lambs among wolves. Do not take a purse or bag or sandals; do not greet anyone on the road. When you enter a house if someone who promotes peace is there, your peace will rest on them; if not, it will return to you. Stay there, eating and drinking whatever they give you, for the worker deserves his wages. Do not move around from house to house. When you enter a town and are welcomed eat what is offered you. Heal the sick who are there and tell them the kingdom of God has come near you. But, when you enter a town and are not welcomed, go into its streets and say 'even the dust of your town we wipe from our feet as a warning to you.' Yet be sure of this, the kingdom of God has come near. I tell you it will be more bearable on that day for Sodom than for that town.' "We were so ready to shake the dust of this town off of our feet and return home.

Our chiropractor, one of the most godly women we'd met in this community, prophesied over us concerning that passage. She said that she felt the Lord was saying to her that there was "something" about the number seventy-two, mentioned in the beginning of the story, when Jesus sent out the seventy-two into the various towns. She said that the Lord was saying that we would sell our home seventy-two days from the day that Jeremy was dismissed. Her prophecy was EXACTLY right. Wow! That was a "goosebumps-raising" experience for us in receiving this personal, supernatural communication from God.

She also mentioned at the same time, that she could see Jeremy being abundantly blessed in the future, and that she could see him on television.

Isaiah 54:17 says "No weapon forged against you will prevail and you will refute every tongue that accuses you." Sure enough, the Lord opened up so many new opportunities for our son. He went back to Carnival and also Royal Caribbean Cruise Lines as an entertainer, and in between contracts, he encountered one opportunity after another to share his passion for praise and worship, song writing and honoring God, as a guest in churches, music festivals, radio and yes, even on television. Recently while playing and singing at a huge retirement community in South Carolina, he was given a check for $500 for ONE of his cds, by a woman who was overwhelmed by God's presence during his presentation.

Chapter Thirty-Six

Think about the passions that you have. God can use them through you to lead others to Christ. I know of a group from a local church who once hit the streets, approaching fast-food restaurants, asking them if they could clean their bathrooms. They became known for awhile, as the "church who cleaned toilets." It was unheard of, and I'll bet that there were employees from those restaurants who visited that church, curious about how God could inspire such love, that they would take pride in doing such menial tasks for Him.

The Lord is not interested in the size of your ministry or the numbers of people you minister to. He is interested in the state of your heart and your desire to serve Him. God said that King David was a man after His own heart. He didn't say that He was a man after His own conquests, strength, power, leadership or talents. It was David's heart that God was blessed by, and we all know that King David took many horrific detours. God does not make mistakes. He does not change His mind when He calls us to a ministry. Romans 11:29 says "For God's gifts and His call are irrevocable." He doesn't give us "limited time only" offers. 1 Timothy 4:14 says "Do not neglect the gift that is in you." 2 Corinthians 4:1 says "Therefore, since through God's mercy we have this ministry, we do not lose heart." When God calls us to serve, He will give us the strength to complete the job.

There will always be detours. Some are self-inflicted and some are God-directed. I left my music ministry for over fourteen years while I "horsed around" at Full Circle Farm, and I know that was God directed. If Jeremy hadn't served in Michigan and if we hadn't followed him there, would I have ever sung or shared my testimony again, as I once did? Maybe not. God knew I needed a new destination in order for me to resume the original ministry He had given to me.

It may be that you, too, might need a new destination, whether it is a move across country or just to a different church down the road, where the environment there will allow you to bloom again. Don't dread it. I think of the precious people I've met and ministered to in my journeys from place to place, who I'd never have met if we'd never ventured outside of our various comfort zones. It's a scary challenge, but if it's orchestrated by the Lord, He will direct you. Joshua 1:9 says "Have I not commanded you? Be strong and courageous. Do not be afraid; do not be discouraged, for the Lord your God will be with you wherever you go." We have no idea of the scope of His purposes and the untold numbers of prayers He answers with just one move of His mighty hand. Romans 11:33-36 says "Oh, the depth of the riches of the wisdom and knowledge of God. How unsearchable His judgments, and His paths beyond tracing out. Who has known the mind of the Lord? Or who has been His counselor? Who has ever given to God that God should repay Him? For from Him and through Him and to Him are all things. To Him be the glory forever! Amen"

Take heart. If you've answered a call to serve the Lord in a specific way in the past and you feel you're on that dreaded detour, don't despair. Call upon the Lord and ask Him to show you His plan. If it's sin that has detoured you, confess it and ask forgiveness. Turn away from your sin. Pour your heart out in prayer. Plunge yourself into His word. Surround yourself with godly friends and counselors.

Chapter Thirty-Seven

T he Bible says that we all have one final destination. Some churches today hesitate to preach on these chilling verses that appear in God's Word. Hebrews 9:27a says "Just as people are destined to die once and after that to face judgment."

Matthew 25:41-46 says "Then He will say to those on His left, 'Depart from Me, you who are cursed, into the eternal fire prepared for the devil and his angels. For I was hungry and you gave me nothing to eat, I was thirsty and you gave me nothing to drink, I was a stranger and you did not invite me in, I needed clothes and you did not clothe me, I was sick and in prison and you did not look after me.' They also will answer Lord, when did we see you hungry or thirsty or a stranger or needing clothes or sick or in prison and did not help you? He will reply, truly I tell you, whatever you did not do for one of the least of these, you did not do for me. Then they will go away to eternal punishment, but the RIGHTEOUS (my emphasis) to eternal life."

Who are these "righteous" that have eternal life that He speaks of? They are those who had given their hearts to Jesus. They did good works out of love, because they had a personal relationship with Him and understood that they already had eternal life. They did not work in order to earn eternal life. There is a huge difference between those two motivations. In

John 14:6 Jesus said "I am the way and the truth and the life. No one comes to the Father except through me." Their ultimate destination was based, not on their good deeds, but on the belief that the death, burial and resurrection of Jesus Christ was to pay for their sins. Ephesians 2:8-9 says "For it is by grace you have been saved, through faith, and this, not from yourselves, it is the gift of God, not by works, so that no one can boast." We cannot work our way to heaven. Jesus did all the work for us.

Heaven is a very real place that we can anticipate with great joy and expectation.1 Corinthians 2:9(KJV) says "But as it is written, eye hath not seen, nor ear heard, neither have entered into the heart of man, the things which God hath prepared for them that love Him." It is a popular saying that there are many paths to heaven, but that is not what the Bible says. Acts 4:12 says "Salvation is found in no one else, for there is no other name under heaven given to mankind by which we must be saved." That name is Jesus. We cannot trust in our intellect, our wealth or our occupations either. Those were given to us by God. James 1:17(NIV) says "Every good and perfect gift is from above, coming down from the Father of the heavenly lights, who does not change like shifting shadows."

Chapter Thirty-Eight

D o you possess a "G.P.S."? I'm talking about a Great Personal Savior! Notice please, that the middle word is "personal." Jesus Christ wants to be your PERSONAL Savior. He wants to have an intimate relationship with YOU. He's given us the Bible, His "grand atlas of road maps," for us to follow so we can find our way through life. He does not wish for us to be lost any longer. He wants us to call upon Him to begin this relationship. Romans 10:13 says "for everyone who calls on the name of the Lord will be saved." I searched for so many years, and I tried everything to fill that empty spot in my heart. Only Jesus, when He filled it, gave me the peace and fulfillment that I had longed for and needed so long.

Please don't allow another moment to go by without inviting Him into your heart and life. Why don't you call on Him right now? You may use this sample prayer below, but He loves to hear you speak to Him in your very own words.

Dear Lord Jesus,

I need You as my personal Savior. I believe You died on the cross to pay the penalty for my sins. I invite You into my life as my Savior and Lord. Thank you for Your free gift of eternal life, which I am claiming today. Help me to begin to build a close, loving relationship with You, beginning right now. In Jesus' name I pray. Amen.

If you just sincerely prayed that prayer, you are now a child of the King of Kings and the Lord of Lords. Hallelujah! Jot down the date. I neglected to do that, and I've always regretted not having a record of the exact date I was so radically saved. You have a new anniversary to celebrate and you'll want to be able to remember just when to do so. Begin to take time to pray and read the Bible daily. Allow Him to speak to you, show you His plans for your life, guide you daily, and give you peace and joy like you've never experienced.

Chapter Thirty-Nine

Linsey and I are now living in Central Virginia on that lovely, downsized farm that we originally dreamed of when we first retired. We see it as another full circle. We have a veggie garden, a gorgeous mountain view, some chickens, two beloved Bernese Mountain dogs, the parrot and two adorable miniature horses, one which pulls a cart. Our menagerie keeps us entertained daily. Both of our horses do hilarious tricks, including Salsa dancing! I have read that many older horse women choose to downsize and collect "miniatures." It's a stage of life called "mini-pause." Ha! It works for me. Our dear Michigan friend, Marilyn thrilled us when she decided to pack up and move to Virginia as well. What a blessing, and what fun we have together. God directed us to a small, country church nearby, that we absolutely love. Marilyn hit the nail on the head when she said that each Sunday feels like a "family reunion." Our pastor is as good a teacher as we have heard anywhere in all of our travels. It's so good to be back in beautiful Bedford County, Virginia. We are loving our life and seeking Him, to see what He has for us to do next.

BEDFORD COUNTY MORNINGS

by Vicki Borders
2009

I woke up to a pink and scarlet sunrise. Despite the sailor's
warning, it was a picture-perfect morning
Grain-filled buckets summon barnyard nickers, snorts
and neighs
There's not a better way to start the day

Thank you, Lord, for Bedford County mornings
It's been a long time coming, haven't always felt this way
Carolina memories aren't so painful now,
Bedford County's really in my heart to stay

The geese are in formation, headed on some lofty mission
And the mountains are a vision, reaching up to touch the sky
The one I love is home today and newfound friends are
on the way
It's going to be another perfect Bedford County day

Thank you, Lord, for Bedford County mornings
It's been a long time coming, haven't always felt this way
Carolina memories aren't so painful now
Bedford County's really in my heart to stay

Don't want to take this kind of gift for granted
Point me to a future friend who's looking for some love
We've got to learn to bloom right where we're planted
Till we're uprooted to our home above

Thank you, Lord, for Bedford County mornings
It's been a long time coming, haven't always felt this way
Carolina memories aren't so painful now
Bedford County's really in my heart to stay
Carolina memories aren't so painful now,
Bedford County's really in my heart to stay

What a journey it's been, from my hippie days, to the CIA, marriage and family, cancer, car wrecks, music and horse ministries. I discover new wrinkles every day. I've experienced a few too many self-inflicted detours, but definitely have encountered one exciting destination after another. As long as the Lord gives me life and health, I'll keep on keeping on. It's not over yet. "Whether you turn to the right or to the left, your ears will hear a voice behind you, saying, 'This is the way; walk in it' Isaiah 30:21. May God bless you bunches and bunches as we travel on together, always looking upward into the face of the One with the nail-scarred hands, our dear Lord and Savior, Jesus Christ. Be sure to honk if you pass us on the highway. We'll probably be following a moving van.

Peace, love and flower power, OH

Vicki, our first anniversary, in Hawaii

Linsey, our first anniversary, in Hawaii

Captain Fox, Vicki and Sherlock, South Bend IN

The Borders family, OH

The Borders family, SC

Our dream farm in beautiful VA

My precious volunteer "daughters"

Working with a sweet group of children

Vicki and Linsey, on Sassy and PJ

Josh, Emily and Ulysses S. Grant

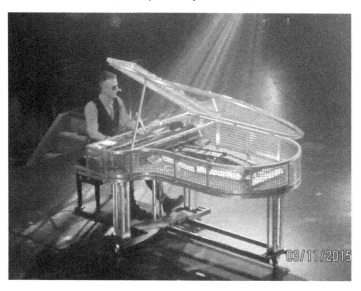

Jeremy entertaining on the cruise ship

Captain Crunch…"Praise the Loooord"!

Mom and her lap warmer, in VA

Adapting to frozen MI

My "illegal" fish!

A too common sight for us

A maxi "full circle" greeting from VA

I would love to hear from you. Feel free to send me an email if this book has been a blessing to you, or if you would like me to pray for any needs you might have. I have been encouraged to record a cd of some of my music, so, with God's provision, I will soon have one available.

My email address is vboldhippy@yahoo.com. Please also check out our son's website at JeremyRayBorders.com

Author Bio

Vicki Borders lives in beautiful Bedford, Virginia, nestled in the Blueridge Mountains. She has been married to Linsey Borders for 47 years and they have two grown sons, a daughter-in-law, and a menagerie. She is a singer/song-writer who has traveled throughout the Southeastern United States sharing her music and life story with churches, at special meetings, and most notably, Stonecroft Ministries. She is an accomplished horsewoman and animal lover. God has opened many doors for her to share the joy she finds in living close to Him, whether in life's valleys or mountaintops.

CPSIA information can be obtained
at www.ICGtesting.com
Printed in the USA
BVHW041732150720
583836BV00009B/283

9 781630 509446